THE LAWYER'S GUIDE TO
Adobe®
Acrobat®
SECOND EDITION

COVERS ADOBE ACROBAT 6.0 and 7.0!

David L. Masters

ABA LawPracticeManagementSection

MARKETING • MANAGEMENT • TECHNOLOGY • FINANCE

Commitment to Quality: The Law Practice Management Section is committed to quality in our publications. Our authors are experienced practitioners in their fields. Prior to publication, the contents of all our books are rigorously reviewed by experts to ensure the highest quality product and presentation. Because we are committed to serving our readers' needs, we welcome your feedback on how we can improve future editions of this book.

Screen shots reprinted with permission from Adobe Systems Incorporated. © 2004 Adobe Systems Incorporated. All rights reserved. Adobe and Adobe Acrobat is/are either (a) registered trademark(s) of Adobe Systems Incorporated in the United States and/or other countries.

Cover design by Jim Colao.

Library of Congress Cataloging-in-Publication Data
The Lawyer's Guide to Adobe® Acrobat®, Second Edition. David L. Masters:
Library of Congress Cataloging-in-Publication Data is on file.

ISBN 1-59031-536-7

09 08 07 06 05   5 4 3 2

Discounts are available for books ordered in bulk. Special consideration is given to state bars, CLE programs, and other bar-related organizations. Inquire at Book Publishing, American Bar Association, 321 N. Clark Street, Chicago, Illinois 60610.

Contents

CHAPTER 13
Plug-ins **123**

CHAPTER 14
Display Mode **131**

CHAPTER 15
E-briefs **139**

CHAPTER 16
Acrobat in the Paperless Office   151

CHAPTER 17
Resources and Glossary   163

About the Author

David Masters is a small-firm general practitioner in Montrose, Colorado. His practice focuses on real estate and business matters, transactions, and litigation, including personal injury, construction law, civil rights, and employment law matters, for both plaintiffs and defendants. He writes and speaks frequently on the use of information technology in the practice of law. Outside the practice of law, he loves to climb mountains.

Mr. Masters has written a new chapter on electronic briefs for the *Colorado Appellate Practice Guide,* published by Continuing Legal Education in Colorado Inc. He has also contributed a chapter on Adobe® Acrobat® to *Flying Solo: A Survival Guide for Solo Lawyers, Fourth Edition,* to be published in 2005 by the ABA Law Practice Management Section.

Mr. Masters received his JD from the University of Montana School of Law in 1986. He is a member of the American Bar Association (1986–present); the ABA Law Practice Management Section (member, ABA TECHSHOW® Planning Board, 2004–2005); the General Practice Solo and Small Firm Section of the Colorado Bar Association (Vice President, District Six, 2003–2005); the Seventh Judicial District Bar Association (1986–present; President, 1990–1992, 1999–2000); West Publishing CD-ROM Advisory Board, 1995; and *The Colorado Lawyer* Board of Editors (1999–2004). He is also a member of the faculty at the National Institute for Trial Advocacy, Rocky Mountain Regional (2001–present), and the adjunct faculty at Mesa State College, Montrose Campus (1992–present).

Acknowledgments

This book would not have been written without the help of my associate, Mindi Conerly, my legal assistant, Jennifer LeBlanc, and our administrative assistant, Barbara Forbes. Jeff Flax deserves credit as the ABA Law Practice Management Section Publishing Board member who persuaded the Section to pursue this project. Thanks to Beverly Loder and the Law Practice Management Section publishing staff for not giving up on me. Finally, thanks to my family for allowing me the additional time to work on this project.

While the author is grateful to Adobe® for creating Acrobat®, there is no sponsorship, affiliation, or endorsement of this book by Adobe Systems Incorporated. The Adobe Acrobat screen shots are reprinted with permission from Adobe Systems Incorporated.

David L. Masters

Introduction

First, I hope this book both inspires and instructs. I hope it inspires you to appreciate the extent to which lawyers manage and process information, and instructs you on how Acrobat can help you make the transition from paper-based to digital information. Second, I hope you enjoy reading this book. Let's face it; it's basically a reference work for a piece of software, and these can be boring.

The transition from paper-based information to digital information has begun. If you are not completely comfortable with conducting legal research electronically, if you are not using a practice-management application, or if you are not conducting 20 percent of your client communication electronically, you are not meeting the current standard of care and are on the road to extinction (with a call to your carrier along the way). As surely as the age of the scrivener has passed, so has the lawyer who relies on paper-based systems to manage and process information.

Lawyers throughout history have adapted to changes in information management: from the scrivener's pen to the clerk's typewriter; from carbon paper to photocopies; from stenographers and shorthand to Dictaphones and transcriptionists; from couriers to guaranteed 9 a.m. overnight delivery; from fax machines to electronic mail.

Even if you don't see yourself on the path toward a paperless office, chances are you've already taken the first steps. If you are using a time and billing program, you have already committed a significant portion of your practice (the income-tracking portion) to the digital realm. If you use a computer to manage your contact and calendar information, then you have taken another step. The next step should be converting client files, discovery documents, and other large collections of paper to digital format. This is not the future—it is the present. After all, we are now in the twenty-first century.

The days of using paper as the substrate for storage and communication of information are waning. As the prominence of paper-based information systems fades, digital systems are on the rise. Working with digital information—storing, organizing, analyzing, retrieving, and delivering it—may sound like a radical departure from your current situation, but it can be done using familiar concepts. The idea here is to take the vast quantities of paper found in almost every law office, convert it to digital form—specifically the ubiquitous Adobe Portable Document Format (PDF)—and use Adobe Acrobat to work with the newly digitized information in ways that are familiar to most lawyers.

Okay, now that I have told you what PDF stands for (Portable Document Format) I need to explain, and seek your indulgence for, the use of "PDF" throughout this book. First, you can see that saying "PDF document" or "PDF format" would be redundant (like ATM machine, HIV virus or VIN number). So, for the most part, I try to use the phrase "PDF file" to refer to collections of pages (documents) that exist in Portable Document Format. You will, no doubt, see the occasional reference to "PDF documents." Please don't be confused and don't hold it against me; we're still dealing with PDF files.

The original (first edition) focus of this book was on Adobe Acrobat version 6.0. Since the first edition was published, Adobe has released Acrobat 7.0. There are enough differences between versions 6.0 and 7.0, in terms of menu commands, keyboard shortcuts, and dialog boxes, to warrant the second edition of this book. The second edition attempts to identify the different menu commands, keyboard shortcuts, and dialog boxes that appear in Acrobat 7.0, so as to keep the content current. As you might expect, Adobe added several new features to Acrobat 7.0. Those new features that are, in my opinion, likely to find use in the average law firm have been included; those that are not likely to be used receive little or no mention (e.g., the 3D Tool). Acrobat should not be confused with Adobe Reader (formerly known as Acrobat Reader). Adobe Reader is a free application that allows anyone to open and print PDF documents, complete Acrobat forms, and do other simple tasks; you cannot *create* PDF documents with Reader. There are many other things you can't do with Reader that you can do with Acrobat; this book focuses on what you can do with Acrobat in the practice of law. Beyond the Adobe family of PDF products (Acrobat, Reader, and so on), other companies sell applications for creating and working with PDF files. Again, the focus here is on Adobe Acrobat versions 6.0 and 7.0.

This book was written to help lawyers use Acrobat to work with digital documents. You should not delegate this task to your staff. Working with digital documents does not require you to become a geek, an IT professional, or anything else. You need only understand and accept that the information on printed pages can be easily captured and displayed on your computer. When you move the information from paper to digital form, few of the ideas and concepts that you currently use to work with the information are lost in the process. Most of them are brought to bear on the information in digital form. This is not rocket science.

The ideas and concepts expressed here are not necessarily unique; for example, the bookmark function was created by Adobe for an obvious purpose, and there are only so many ways that bookmarks can be added to PDF documents. That said, the how and why of bookmarks in the legal realm merits discussion. For example, with Acrobat you can take fifty documents, put them together in a single file, and bookmark each. Now, if those fifty documents happen to be trial exhibits, you have just created an electronic exhibit notebook with a hyperlinked (those click-and-go-there things common to Web pages) table of contents. The contents of this exhibit notebook can be replicated across multiple computer systems, transferred by electronic means, and even displayed in the courtroom using a digital projector. But in the end, it's just an exhibit notebook.

This book was based on one small law firm's experience using Acrobat to develop a virtually paperless office. Over the course of several years, we found Acrobat to be more and more useful, to the point that we felt a book was called for. This book is aimed at both newcomers to Acrobat and experienced users alike. This book should be helpful in putting Acrobat to use in any law practice, whether the practice is transactional or litigation oriented. There may be a limit on Acrobat's usefulness in large firms. As a lawyer who has never practiced in a firm with more than six lawyers, I'll leave it to you to imagine what I mean by large firms.

For the most part, the chapters of the book are independent from one another. That said, Chapters 1 and 2 cover some background information about the *what* and *why* of PDF. Chapter 3 covers the basics of using Acrobat, from a description of the work area to how to navigate within PDF documents. New users may need to spend some time familiarizing themselves with Acrobat, or at least refer back to these initial chapters from time to time. The book should serve as a reference for Acrobat functions useful in the law office. For example, if a user wants information about creating PDFs from Web pages, then only Chapter 12 need be consulted. The book does not attempt to catalog and describe every feature and function of Acrobat. That task has been done by Adobe in the Acrobat online Help manual, and there are a number of books that detail advanced uses of Acrobat (see Chapter 17, "Resources and Glossary").

Finally, I have no personal or financial interest in Adobe or Acrobat. Indeed, Adobe expressed no interest in publishing this book (they did approve the screen shots as required by the Acrobat End User License Agreement). As you will see, I think Acrobat is a great product that will be the next big thing in the realm of legal technology.

That said, even great products have weak points. Some "improvements" from one version to the next are (in my opinion) a step backward. Unless we (you and I) can convince the software company to return prior functions that are dropped or crippled in the move to "advance" software, complaining about these changes amounts to no more than crying over spilt milk; we might as well accept the changes and get on with our work.

Why PDF?

Information is the lawyer's stock in trade. Lawyers process information. Historically, much of the information processed by lawyers has existed in paper form. As times have changed, so has the format of information. Today, much information exists in digital form, and much remains in paper. Digital information can be stored, manipulated, analyzed, and managed much more effectively and efficiently than information maintained in paper format. Someday, the vast majority of information will be created and maintained in digital format. In the meantime, the information that comes to lawyers on paper can be converted to digital format.

To convert paper-based information to digital information, you much first choose a digital format. Formats vary in what tools are available for working with the files, and how easily and universally the files can be shared with other people. With Acrobat, you can easily convert paper documents to digital files and then work with them in many different ways. You can also convert other digital file types, such as word processing files or spreadsheets. Virtually any file that can be printed on paper can be converted to PDF. Acrobat does more than just allow you to work with digital documents in the same ways you work with paper documents. It does not, however, replace your word processing application (such as Microsoft Word, Corel WordPerfect, and so on).

Digital information can exist in many formats. Just as paper bearing information may be bound in books or jotted on the backs of cocktail napkins, and be written in many different languages, digital information can exist in a variety of media and formats (although the choice of format is more important than the choice of medium). Converting existing stocks of paper-based information into digital information also requires a choice of image format. Today, common image formats include JPEG, TIFF, and PDF. The choice of format appears to have been made: courts and government institutions have chosen PDF.

PDF has become the de facto standard for the secure and reliable distribution and exchange of electronic documents, and has a proven track record. PDF is a universal file format that preserves the fonts, images, graphics, and layout of any source document, regardless of the application and platform used to create it. PDF files are compact and complete, and can be shared, viewed, and printed by anyone with the free Adobe Reader program. To date, more than 500 million copies of Reader have been distributed.

You can use Acrobat to convert, create, distribute, and exchange secure and reliable PDF documents (you cannot create PDF documents using Reader). There are alternatives to Acrobat for the creation of PDF files, such as 1-Step RoboPDF, absolutePDF Creator Easy, activePDF Composer, and Pdf995, to name a few (**www.planetpdf.com** lists almost three hundred tools under the category "Creation & Conversion").

Governments and enterprises around the world have adopted PDF to streamline document management, increase productivity, and reduce reliance on paper. For example, PDF is the standard format for the electronic submission of drug approvals to the U.S. Food and Drug Administration (FDA). The federal courts are adopting a new electronic case management and electronic case files system (CM/ECF). It provides federal courts with enhanced and updated docket management and allows them to maintain case documents in electronic form. Some courts allow case documents (pleadings, motions, petitions) to be filed with the court over the Internet. CM/ECF implementation in the bankruptcy courts has been underway since early 2001. The federal CM/ECF program stores all documents as PDF files. District court implementation of CM/ECF began in 2002, and appellate court implementation is scheduled to begin in late 2004. In state courts, the LexisNexis File & Serve system has been adopted by courts in eleven states.* Like the federal CM/ECF sys-

---

*Courts using the LexisNexis File & Serve system: Arizona (Maricopa County Superior Court, Pima County Superior Court); California (Alameda County, San Diego, San Francisco, Shasta County); Colorado (District and County Courts—statewide); Delaware (Court of Chancery, Superior Courts—statewide); District of Columbia (D.C. Superior Court, D.C. Contract Appeals Board); Georgia (Dekalb County Superior Court, Fulton County State, Fulton County Superior); Illinois (DuPage 18th Judicial Circuit Court); Maryland (Baltimore City Circuit Court); Michigan (Ottawa County, 20th Judicial Circuit Court); New Jersey (Atlantic County Superior Court); Ohio (Butler County Court of Common Pleas, Cuyahoga County Court of Common Pleas, Lucas County Court of Common Pleas); Pennsylvania (Lancaster County Court of Common Pleas); Texas (Jefferson County District Courts, Montgomery County District Courts); Washington (Chelan County Superior Court).

tem, LexisNexis File & Serve maintains all documents as PDF files. PDF is also used by the governments of the United Kingdom and Germany for electronic document exchange.

An open file-format specification, PDF is available to anyone who wants to develop tools to create, view, or manipulate PDF documents. Indeed, more than 1,800 vendors offer PDF-based solutions, ensuring that law firms that adopt the PDF standard have a variety of tools to customize document processes. Lawyers can distribute rich-media PDF slide shows created using Adobe Photoshop Album software, and anyone with Reader can view them. Such slide shows can be a powerful enhancement to electronic briefs or settlement brochures.

Acrobat provides good image-acquisition capabilities, including the ability to perform optical character recognition (OCR) while retaining an exact image of the scanned pages. Recent versions of Word and WordPerfect contain drivers to publish word processing files to PDF. Because PDF is an open standard, companies like Corel and Microsoft can develop and include PDF tools in their software applications.

Besides acquiring images, Acrobat makes PDF files truly useful. For example, bookmarks and sticky notes can be added to image-only files. If the files have a text background, the text can be formatted with highlighting, strike-throughs, or underlining. PDF files with background text can be searched; image-only files cannot be searched but information contained in the Document Summary or in attached notes is included in indexes of document collections. PDF documents can be reviewed and annotated; the annotation can be summarized and published to PDF with just a few keystrokes or mouse clicks.

Acrobat allows lawyers to work with digital documents in much the same way they work with paper documents. That does not mean that Acrobat replaces your word processor. Just as you cannot effectively edit a paper document, you cannot effectively edit documents using Acrobat. You can mark them up, like you would a paper document, but the real work of editing remains the domain of word processing applications. While Acrobat adheres to many of the familiar techniques we employ to work with paper-based documents, it allows lawyers to work with digital documents more efficiently, more effectively, and with greater mobility. With a scanner and Acrobat, any law office can become a paperless office. The person that does the paper filing becomes the person who scans incoming documents. When documents are scanned and saved they are "filed." For more information on how Acrobat can provide the foundation for a paperless office, see Chapter 16 "Acrobat in the Paperless Office."

PDF Document Types   **2**

Not all PDF documents are created equally. There are image-only PDFs and image-on-text files. Understanding the fundamental difference between image-only and image-on-text files is absolutely critical; a short explanation of the difference appears more than once throughout this book. Regardless of whether you work with image-only or image-on-text files, the image remains an exact duplicate of the original paper-based document.

§ 2.1 Image-Only Files

Image-only PDFs are just that—images only, just digital photocopies of paper documents. Think of image-only PDF files as pages in a notebook; you can look at the pages but you cannot search the notebook without reading each page. Even though image-only files cannot be searched, they are still more useful than a notebook full of paper pages. Using Acrobat, image-only files can be annotated with comments and graphics. Comments can be summarized (see Chapter 7, "Commenting Tools") and comment content can be searched with Windows Explorer.

§ 2.2 Image-on-Text Files

Image-on-text files have an exact image of the paper copy, with text behind the image. Image-on-text files are created by printing an existing computer file to PDF (word processing and spreadsheet files are good examples), or by running a PDF image-only file through an OCR application. When using OCR applications, care must be taken to select a final file type that produces an exact image on text; otherwise, the visible text in the PDF image may be changed to comport with the interpretation of the OCR application. Acrobat 6.0 has the built-in ability to OCR PDF documents; Acrobat calls this function Paper Capture. For more information on creating and working with image-on-text files, see Chapter 10, "Searching and Indexing."

An entirely separate program, Adobe Acrobat Capture, is an industrial-strength tool that teams with your scanner to convert volumes of paper documents into PDF files. Accurate OCR, advanced page and content recognition, powerful cleanup tools, and batch processing allow you to turn paper-based information into high-quality electronic documents image-on-text PDF files. For more information about Adobe Acrobat Capture, go to **http://www.adobe .com/products/acrcapture/main.html**.

Image-on-text PDF files are the holy grail of legal document management. When paper documents are scanned to other image formats such as TIFF or JPEG, only a digital image of the paper exists. If characters that comprise that image are converted to text, the conversion process inevitably changes the appearance of the text in the image file. Not so with PDF files; the image remains an exact duplicate of the original while the interpreted text exists independently behind, or a layer below, the image. The text file behind or below the image can be searched. Depending on the quality of the paper documents scanned, thousands of pages can be captured as exact copies and made searchable through the use of OCR applications. There are limits and caveats with OCR technology that are discussed in more detail in chapter 10. (See Section 10.2, "OCR Quality Experiment.")

Getting Started

3

Before looking at specific features of Acrobat, and how those features might be used in the practice of law, we need to take some time to become familiar with the application that makes working with digital documents as comfortable and familiar as working with paper-based documents. To start with, Acrobat comes in three varieties: Reader, Standard, and Professional. Reader is free, and with it anyone can open, display, search, and print PDF documents. Reader does not allow you to add bookmarks, notes, links, or most of the other features that make Acrobat a valuable tool in the law office. Acrobat Standard and Professional are the "full" versions of the program and are the applications for working with PDF documents. The primary difference between the Standard and Professional versions has to do with creating PDF forms; the Standard version does not create forms while the Professional version does. Having the ability to create forms can virtually eliminate the need for a typewriter in the law office. You can scan any document to PDF, then create form fields that can be filled in and printed.

Acrobat looks much like any other software application (such as a word processor, spreadsheet, or database manager). If you make Acrobat fill the entire display on your computer you are looking at the work area (Figure 3.1).

The work area has a number of components such as menus, toolbars, the navigation pane and the lower button bar. The large area in the middle displays PDF documents; for the most part this is where the action takes place. Before moving on to describing the action, take a look at the various components of the work area and how tasks are described in this book.

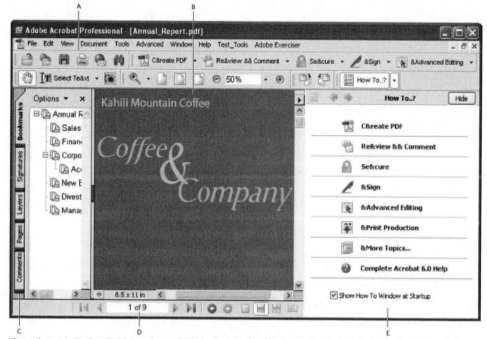

The work area A. Toolbars B. Document pane C. Navigation pane (Bookmarks tab displayed) D. Status bar E. How To window

Figure 3.1

§ 3.1 Menus

Many Acrobat tasks can be performed through menu selections. Menus are the topmost row of items in the Acrobat window. There are eight menus: **File, Edit, View, Document, Tools, Advanced, Window,** and **Help.** Figure 3.2 shows the **Tools** menu pulled down and extended to display the highlighting tools.

Throughout this book as tasks are described, the menu commands are listed and in some cases illustrated. Menu commands list the sequence of items to be selected and appear as follows:

Menu (Edit Preferences): **Edit** > **Preferences**

If a difference exists for a menu command between Acrobat Versions 6.0 and 7.0, both will be listed, preceded by the appropriate version number. If no difference exists, then the menu command works as shown in versions 6.0 and 7.0. The menu description states, in parentheses, the task to be accomplished (shown above as Edit Preferences), followed by the menu to select (shown above as Edit), followed by the item or items to be selected in sequence from the menu (shown above as Preferences). The first menu item is followed by ">," then the next item to be selected is listed. Some menus are several levels

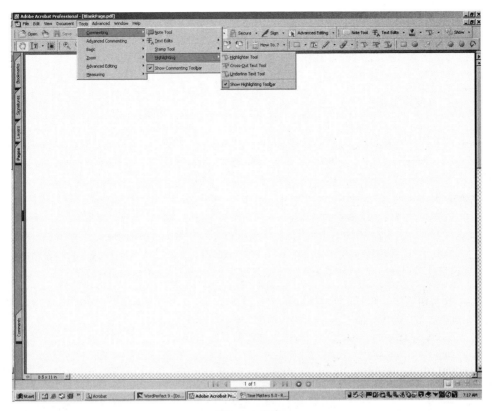

Figure 3.2

deep. In those cases, the menu items are separated by ">" in the order that they are to be selected.

When it is possible to execute menu commands by a series of keystrokes, those shortcuts follow the menu description and are shown as follows:

Keystroke (Edit Preferences): **Alt+E** or **Ctrl+K**

If a difference exists for a keystroke command between Acrobat Versions 6.0 and 7.0, both will be listed, preceded by the appropriate version number. If no difference exists, then the keystroke command works as shown in versions 6.0 and 7.0. The keystroke descriptions throughout this book use the following conventions:

- ◆ **Alt** refers to the Alt key
- ◆ **Ctrl** refers to the Ctrl (or Control) key
- ◆ **Shift** refers to the Shift key
- ◆ When the plus symbol (+) appears between key references, the keys must be pressed simultaneously (for example, **Shift+Ctrl+N** means hold down the Shift, Control, and N keys all at the same time)
- ◆ When a hyphen (-) appears between key references, the keys are pressed in sequence

Menu selections, icons, tools, checkboxes, dialogs, tabs, and other items that appear on your screen and that you interact with when executing commands are shown in **bold type.**

§ 3.2 Toolbars

In addition to menus and keystrokes, some Acrobat tasks can be performed by clicking an icon on one of the toolbars. Indeed, some tasks can be performed only by clicking on a toolbar icon. Acrobat opens with a set of default toolbars; more specialized and advanced toolbars can be displayed at your command. Some special or advanced toolbars "float" in the work area, or can be docked with the other toolbars. Figure 3.3 shows the Create PDF toolbar.

You can display some or all toolbars. To quickly display all toolbars, right-click in the toolbar area and select **Dock All Toolbars,** or

Menu (dock all toolbars): **View** > **Toolbars** > **Dock All Toolbars**
6.0 Keystroke (dock all toolbars): **Alt+Ctrl+D**
6.0 Keystroke (dock all toolbars): **Alt+V-T-D**
or
7.0 Keystroke (dock all toolbars): **Ctrl+F8**

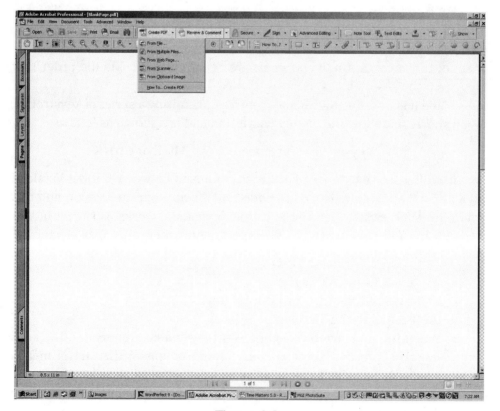

Figure 3.3

To quickly hide all of the toolbars press the F8 key. This can be handy if you need maximum display real estate, such as when you have a word processing application and Acrobat open side by side on the screen. Why would you want to do that? It's just like looking at your draft answer (the word processing document) next to the complaint (PDF file). You can go through paragraph-by-paragraph and compare the answers to the allegations in the complaint. When you want to see the toolbars again, just press F8 and they will return. If you forget that F8 will hide and show the toolbars, the same result can be achieved through the View menu.

Menu (Hide/Show Toolbars): **View** > **Toolbars** > **Hide Toolbars/Show Toolbars**
Keystroke (Show/Hide Toolbars): **F8**

§ 3.3 The Navigation Panes

A principal attribute that recommends Acrobat for use in the legal profession is the ability to navigate through PDF documents in much the same way as you would browse through a file folder or notebook full of paper. But you can navigate through PDF documents with Acrobat in more ways than you can with a paper file; Acrobat provides a number of ways. One way is by using the Navigation tabs located on the left side of the document window (visible in Figures 3.2 and 3.3 above).

The tabs are **Bookmarks, Signatures, Layers, Pages,** and **Comments.** The Bookmarks, Pages, and Comments tabs are useful navigation tools for lawyers using Acrobat; Layers and Signatures may not be as useful. Clicking on one of the tabs displays the navigation pane for that type of navigational aid. For example, clicking on the **Bookmarks** navigation tab displays the bookmarks pane. If the document contains bookmarks they are displayed in the navigation pane. The same goes for comments. (The **Pages** tab always displays all the pages in the document). Clicking on any one of the bookmarks (or comments if that tab was selected) takes you to the point in the document where the bookmark (or comment) was created. If the document does not contain bookmarks or comments, then the respective navigation panes are empty.

§ 3.4 Basic Navigation

Basic navigation of PDFs can be achieved by simply paging through the document. Another simple mode of navigation is going to a specific page number. More sophisticated navigation involves using Bookmarks, Links, Comments, or Thumbnail views. Paging through a document calls to mind turning pages in a book or file; you can turn forward or backward one page at a time. To navigate through a document one page at a time, use the Previous Page and Next Page buttons on the button bar at the bottom of the document window (the arrows directly to the left and right of the page number), or use the **Page Up** and **Page Down** keys on your keyboard. Note: this only works when the document is displayed in the Fit Page view; if it is displayed in Actual Size or Fit Width, pressing **Page Up** or **Page Down** first moves the document in the window up or down some distance before moving to the next or previous page. To jump to the beginning or end of a document, use the First Page and Last Page buttons located on the button bar at the bottom of the document window adjacent to the Previous Page and Next Page buttons, or use the keyboard command **Ctrl+Home** and **Ctrl+End** respectively. To browse forward or backward in a document, one page at a time, use the following commands:

Menu (Go to next or previous page): **View** > **Go To** > **Next Page** (or **Previous Page**)

Keystroke (Go to next or previous page): **Page Up** (or **Page Down**) Note: this only works when with the document is displayed in the Fit Page view; if displayed in Actual Size or Fit Width, pressing **Page Up** or **Page Down** first moves the document in the window up or down some distance before moving to the next or previous page. Note: except when the Select Text Tool is active, the Left Arrow Key will move back one page and the Right Arrow Key will move forward one page. When the Select Text Tool is active, the arrow keys move the cursor.

Specific pages can be located by using the Go To function:

Menu (Go To Page *n*): **View** > **Go To** > **n** (insert page number *n*)
Keystroke (Go To Page *n*): **Alt+V-G-*n*** (insert page number *n*)
Keystroke (Go To Page *n*): **Shift+Ctrl+*n*** (insert page number *n*)

Your navigational course within a document or across multiple documents can be retraced by using the View buttons at the bottom of the document window, Next View and Previous View, which are adjacent to the Page buttons. As with most other tasks in Acrobat, the Next View and Previous View can also be achieved using menu commands or keyboard commands:

Menu (Go To Previous/Next View): **View** > **Go To** > **Previous View** (or **Next View**)

Keystroke (Go To Previous/Next View): **Alt+Left Arrow** (or **Alt+Right Arrow**)

When navigating through documents by paging through or using bookmarks, the View buttons may receive little use. But when navigating by way of links, the View buttons become indispensable. When you click on a link, the quickest way back to the point where you clicked is by clicking the Previous View button. Think of the View buttons as comparable to the Forward and Back buttons in browsers like Netscape and Internet Explorer.

§ 3.5 Bookmarks

Bookmarks are like a table of contents, except that clicking on a bookmark takes you to a predetermined page within a PDF document. Bookmarks may be one of the most powerful features of PDF documents for lawyers. As you page through a document, bookmarks can be added with the keystroke **Ctrl+B**, followed by typing a short name for the bookmark. Bookmarks can be nested (arranged in a hierarchy) and differentiated by font style (plain, bold, italics, or bold and italic) or font color. The creation and use of bookmarks is discussed in more detail in Chapter 6, "Adding Document Navigation Aids."

Think of the basic four-part file folder: with the center section turned to the right, pages containing your notes may be on the left and correspondence on the right; flip the center section to the left and miscellaneous documents may be on the left and pleadings on the right. If the entire file contents were a single PDF document, then you could have four main bookmarks for notes, correspondence, miscellaneous, and pleadings. Under each of the main categories you could have bookmarks for each of the individual documents (such as a separate bookmark for each item of correspondence). Using a standard four-part file folder as an example of how bookmarks might be used provides a good illustration, but is probably not the best practice. It would be better to have a folder (directory) representing the paper file folder that contained subfolders (subdirectories) for each of the types of documents (notes, correspondence, miscellaneous, and pleadings). A discussion of digital filing systems appears in Chapter 16, "Acrobat in the Paperless Office."

§ 3.6 Links

Links in PDF documents are like hyperlinks in Web pages. Clicking on a link takes you to a new location. Links can take you to a specific page in the current document, to the first page of another document, to a specific page in another document, or to a Web site; they can open another file type, play audio or video, and more. The creation and use of links is discussed in more detail in Chapter 6, "Adding Document Navigation Aids." Links are the essence of electronic briefs, discussed in Chapter 15, "E-briefs."

§ 3.7 Views

Acrobat displays document pages in a variety of views. The default view can be set in **Edit** > **Preferences.** When you look at a piece of paper in a file folder or notebook, you typically see the entire page. You might use a ruler or sheet of paper to cover portions of the page so that you can focus on specific areas. The three primary views in Acrobat are Actual Size, Fit Page, and Fit Width.

◆ Actual Size view displays the current page proportionally within the document window. The amount of the page that you see depends on the capabilities of the computer and your display settings. To display the current document in Actual Size, click on the **Actual Size** icon on the toolbar, or:

Menu (View Actual Size): **View** > **Actual Size**
Keystroke (View Actual Size): **Ctrl+1**

◆ Fit Page view displays the full current page from top to bottom. On smaller monitors it may be difficult to read the text on the page displayed, but this may be the preferred view for browsing through a document (you can always zoom in). To display the current document in Fit Page view, click on the **Fit Page** icon on the toolbar, or:

Menu (Fit Page View): **View** > **Fit Page**
Keystroke (Fit Page View): **Ctrl+2**

◆ Fit Width view displays the current page at maximum width. This view always chops off the bottom of the page, making it necessary to use the Page Down key, the scroll bar, or the scroll wheel on your pointing device to see the bottom of the page. If you need to read the text of a document this may be the best view because it provides the largest image that can be viewed with the least amount of scrolling (Fit Width does not require any side-to-side scrolling that may be necessary if the view is zoomed in closer than page width). To display the current document in Fit Width view, click on the **Fit View** icon on the toolbar, or:

Menu (Fit Width View): **View** > **Fit Width**
Keystroke (Fit Width View): **Ctrl+3**

In addition to the three primary views, Acrobat includes the ability to zoom in (magnify) or zoom out (reduce). Zooming becomes important if you work with large-format documents such as survey maps or plats, or are concerned with the fine print or fine markings in a standard-size document. When a 24-inch by 36-inch survey map has been scanned or printed to PDF and displayed on your monitor, what you see is substantially smaller than the original document (unless, of course, you have a 42-inch monitor). For example, a 24 x 36 survey plat displayed in Fit Page mode is reduced to 35 percent of its actual size. But not to worry—Acrobat can zoom in (magnify) to an incredible 6,400 percent. To zoom the view in or out from the current display:

Menu (Zoom In or Out): **View** > **Zoom To** [select the desired magnification or view]

Keystroke (Zoom In or Out): **Ctrl+M** [select the desired magnification or view]

In addition to the zoom features available through the menus or keystrokes, Acrobat has a dynamic zoom tool that lets the user zoom in or out simply by holding down the left mouse or pointer button and dragging the mouse or pointer up or down. The amount of zoom (magnification or reduction) is displayed in the Zoom toolbar as a percentage. The dynamic zoom tool is one of those things that you can use only by clicking the tool icon on the toolbar. When you are done examining the area of the document that you zoomed in on, simply click on the preferred view button in the toolbar (Actual Size, Full Page, or Fit Width). The dynamic zoom can be a powerful tool for examining documents using a digital projector in settlement conferences, depositions, or the courtroom. Note, however, that the dynamic zoom tool does not work in Full Screen view (this is discussed below).

Acrobat also has a display feature called Full Screen view. This display option presents each page in Fit Page mode and removes the work area from the display so that the page displayed is all that you see (except for a black or color border that fills the rest of the screen). Full Screen view works well for slide show type presentations, or even the presentation of evidence, but because all of the tools are hidden you cannot zoom in or out or add comments to the displayed image. To activate the Full Screen view:

Menu (Activate Full Screen View): **Window** > **Full Screen View**
Keystroke (Activate Full Screen View): **Ctrl+L**

To exit Full Screen view, press the **Esc** key. For more information on using Full Screen view, see Chapter 14, "Display Mode."

§ 3.8 Preferences

Preferences, or default operating conditions, can be set from the Edit menu. For example, if you prefer to have documents open in the Fit Page view, this can be set as an operating default.

Menu (Edit Preferences): **Edit** > **Preferences**
Keystroke (Edit Preferences): **Ctrl+K**

The Preferences dialog box presents a bewildering list of options that can be set, more than can be described here (see Figure 3.4 for the Version 6.0 Preferences dialog box; see Figure 3.5 for the Version 7.0 Preferences dialog box). Go to the Preferences window and explore. When in doubt, consult the Help menu.

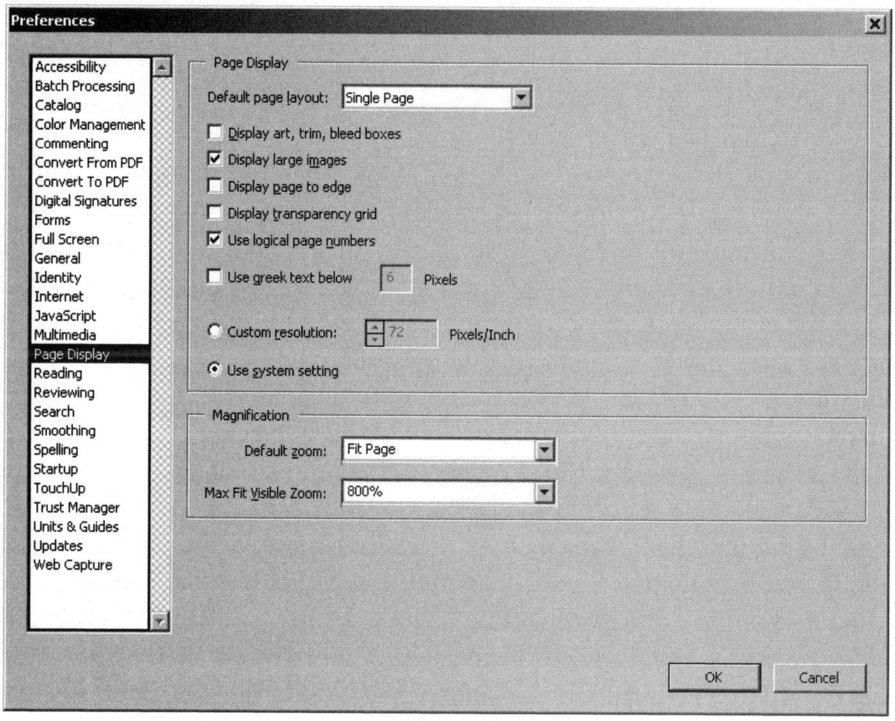

Figure 3.4

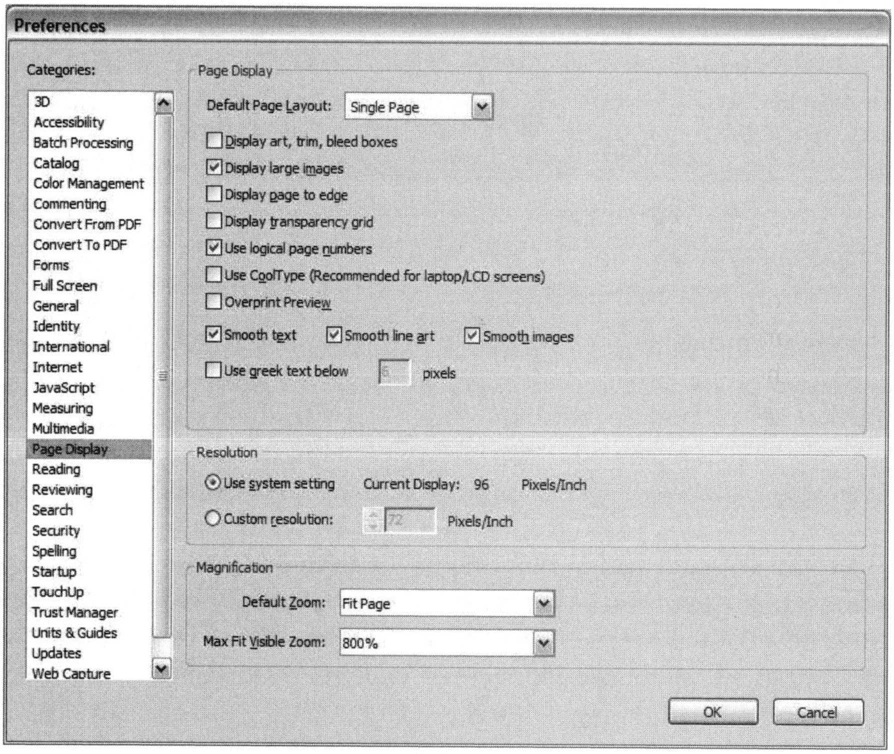

Figure 3.5

Creating PDF Files

4

PDF files can be created by using Acrobat to "print" to PDF, by scanning to PDF, by converting existing files, and by capturing Web pages. Using Acrobat as a standard tool in the law office, on par with a word processing application, is no longer just beneficial—it is approaching the level of necessity. Just as law firms depend on word processing applications to create documents, lawyers are depending on Acrobat to create PDFs and work with them. With various state and federal courts implementing (and in some cases mandating) e-filing, basic knowledge of creating and working with PDF files has become as necessary as proficiency in using a word processor.

PDF is an excellent choice for the law office because it preserves the fonts, formatting, and graphics of the source file, regardless of the application and platform used to create it. A variety of file formats can be converted to PDF. For instance, a set of interrogatories can be created in WordPerfect or Word, printed to PDF, and then e-mailed to opposing counsel or the client. Likewise, a spreadsheet prepared using Excel or QuattroPro can be printed to PDF and e-mailed as an attachment to someone who does not have the source application software to open or read an Excel or QuattroPro file. PDF files are compact and can be exchanged, viewed, navigated, and printed by anyone with the free Adobe Reader software, and the document integrity is maintained. In addition to creating PDF files from virtually any software application, you can also create PDF files by scanning and capturing paper documents and by downloading and converting Web pages.

The File menu of most word processing applications includes a New option. Selecting New creates a blank document in a new window. There is no New option in the Acrobat File menu; instead, you are given the option to Create PDF from an existing file, scanned document, or Web page, or by converting a file that already exists in another format. (Note: not all file formats can be converted to PDF using this feature.)

As mentioned above, one of the main benefits to using PDF in the law office is the ease with which you can convert a word processing or other document simply by printing it to PDF. To print PDF documents you need a PDF printer (which is software, not hardware). Acrobat installs a single PDF printer, Adobe PDF (Acrobat 5.0 installed two such printers, PDFWriter and Distiller). Adobe PDF is like any other printer driver, but it writes out PDF files instead of printer commands. The Adobe PDF printer appears in the Windows Printers folder and is available to all applications that use associated Windows printers (see Figure 4.1).

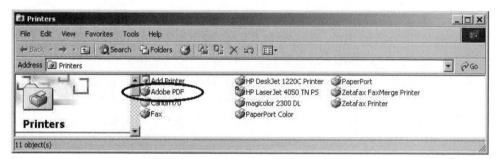

Figure 4.1

The default Acrobat installation adds three Convert to Adobe PDF buttons to the toolbar in Microsoft Word, Excel, and PowerPoint that allow you to create PDF files quickly and easily from within those applications. Adobe PDF is also added to the menu bar. By default, PDF files created using these commands and buttons preserve hyperlinks, styles, and bookmarks present in the source file. In Windows XP, if the Convert to Adobe PDF buttons are not visible in the Microsoft application, choose **View** > **Toolbars** > **PDFMaker 6.0.**

Another incredible benefit of using PDF in the law office is the ability to scan all the information that comes into the law office in paper format and save it on your hard disk drive (or better still, on a drive shared over a local area network). Once you become comfortable with Acrobat, you are on your way to operating a paperless office.

§ 4.1 Creating PDFs Using the Print Command

The most common way to create PDF documents from existing files is to use the Print to PDF function. As mentioned earlier, Acrobat installs a Convert to PDF button on the toolbars of Microsoft Word, Excel, and PowerPoint. A Publish to PDF button can be installed on the toolbar in WordPerfect (version 9.0 and later). If you have a Print, Publish, or Convert to PDF button on the toolbar, you need only click it to start the process. Otherwise, to print a document to PDF:

1. Open the file that you want to convert to an Adobe PDF file in its authoring application, and choose **File** > **Print.**
2. Choose **Adobe PDF** (or **PDFWriter** or **Distiller**) from the list of printers.
3. From the **Print** dialog box, click **OK.**

By default, the PDF file is saved in the same directory as the source file, using the same filename, but with a .pdf extension. The conversion of files to PDF also uses the printer settings or page setup you have chosen for the application that created the file. For example, if you are using Microsoft Power-Point and choose Handouts from the print dialog box, the resulting PDF file is based on the Handouts version of the presentation.

§ 4.2 Creating PDFs Using a Scanner

Perhaps the ultimate utility of Acrobat is the ability to convert paper documents into digital PDF files using a scanner. Discovery documents, incoming mail, and pleadings can all be converted to digital files using Acrobat and a scanner. To create a PDF document using a scanner:

1. Place the document to be scanned in the scanner, then click the **Create PDF** button and select **From Scanner**; alternatively, use the menu or keyboard commands shown below.
   Menu (Create PDF from Scanner): **File** > **Create PDF** > **From Scanner**
   6.0 Keystroke (Create PDF from Scanner): **Alt+F-F-N**
   7.0 Keystroke (Create PDF from Scanner): **Alt+F-F-S**
2. In the **Create PDF From Scanner** dialog box, select your scanner device. Choose the format (single-sided or double-sided) and specify whether to create a new PDF document or append the converted scan to the currently open PDF document. Check the compatibility level. In general, compatibility with the most recent version of Acrobat yields a small file size; however, problems arise when sharing documents with those who have older versions. By default, pages are compressed for compactness and edge shadows are removed.
3. Click **Scan.** At this point a new dialog box appears that allows selection of additional scanning options such as paper size and the type of file to be created (color, gray scale, or black and white). This dialog box is a function of the software that came with the scanner (the scanner driver) and its contents vary depending on the make and model of scanner used. Accordingly, its precise contents cannot be described

here. However, unless you need a color or gray-scale image of the paper document, always select black-and-white (sometimes listed as text). Documents scanned as black-and-white images produce substantially smaller PDF files sizes compared to documents scanned as color or gray-scale images.

4. Click **Next** if you are scanning multiple pages to the same file; click **Done** when finished scanning.

The document scanned to PDF is now visible in the work area of the Acrobat window. At this point the document must be saved to an appropriate location on the local computer or network. To save the newly created PDF document:

Menu (Save File): **File** > **Save**
Keystroke (Save File): **Alt+F-S** or,
Keystroke (Save File): **Ctrl+S**

§ 4.3 Creating PDFs Using Drag and Drop

PDF files can be created by dragging the native application file into the document pane of the Acrobat window or onto the Acrobat icon. This can be particularly useful for converting large format graphic files such as survey plats or maps that have been scanned to TIFF or JPEG by an outside service.

To convert files to PDF by dragging and dropping, drag the file into the open Acrobat window or onto the Acrobat icon.

Note: if you have a file open in the Acrobat window and you drag a file into the document pane, the converted file opens as a new PDF file. Once the conversion has taken place the new PDF document appears in the document window; save it to an appropriate location on the local computer or network.

§ 4.4 Creating PDFs Using File Conversion

A number of file types can be converted to PDF using this feature. Notably, WordPerfect files are not presently among the file types that can be converted. For the most part, only image files (.jpg, .tif, etc.) and files from Microsoft applications can be converted using this feature. To convert an existing file to PDF:

Click the **Create PDF** button and select **From File;** alternatively, use the menu or keyboard commands shown below.
Menu (Create PDF from File): **File** > **Create PDF** > **From File**
Keystroke (Create PDF from File): **Alt+F-F-F**

To create a single PDF from multiple files, click the Create PDF button and select From Multiple Files; alternatively, use the following menu or keyboard commands:

Menu (Create PDF From Multiple Files): **File** > **Create PDF** > **From Multiple Files**
Keyboard (Create PDF From Multiple Files): **Alt+F-F-M**

Whether creating a PDF from a single file or from multiple files, the source file(s) that you selected will be converted (printed) to PDF. By default, the PDF file created from a single file will be saved in the same directory as the source file, with the same name as the original, but with a .pdf extension. The PDF file created from multiple source files will have the default name of "Binder.pdf." Creating a single PDF from multiple source files is easy and a real time saver when your client brings you a hundred digital photographs or opposing counsel delivers discovery documents as TIFF files.

§ 4.5 Creating PDFs from Web Pages

Creating PDF documents from Web pages comes in handy when you want to capture an entire section of a Web site, such as a code section or reported decision. You can also save electronic statements, receipts, and Web orders directly to PDFs. Web pages can be converted to PDF directly from Internet Explorer with a single click. PDFs created from Web pages can include active links from the pages, depending on the number of levels captured (Get Only n levels). If the linked pages are not included in the PDF, Acrobat prompts the user to open the pages in a browser (in other words, connect to the Internet and open the page in your default browser). Web pages captured to PDF have their Macromedia Flash content preserved (those sometimes annoying moving elements in Web pages). This is possible because the PDF file format itself has been upgraded (to version 1.5). This new format supports JPEG2000 image compression and can fully embed multimedia content instead of linking to external audio and movie files.

To create a PDF document from a Web page:

Click the **Create PDF** button and select **From Web Page;** alternatively, use the menu or keyboard commands shown below.
Menu (Create PDF from Web Page): **File** > **Create PDF** > **From Web Page**
Keystroke (Create PDF from Web Page): **Alt+F-F-W**

The **Create PDF from Web Page** dialog box appears with a space to enter the URL (Web address) for the desired Web page (Figure 4.2).

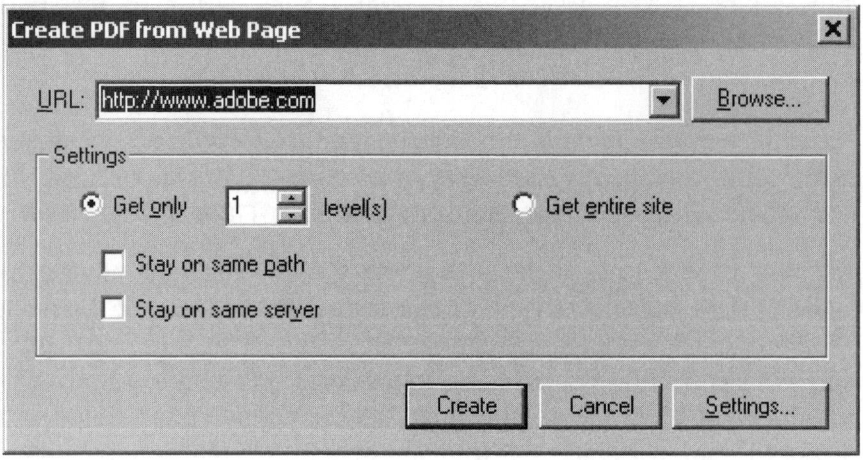

Figure 4.2

You may find it easiest to locate the Web page in the browser of your choice, then highlight the URL in the browser address window and copy it to the clipboard (**Edit** > **Copy** or **Ctrl+C**). Now you can paste the URL into the Acrobat **Create PDF from Web Page** dialog box. Notice that the dialog box has other options for you to select. You can specify the number of levels to convert or even select an entire site (use the latter with caution—telling Acrobat to convert the entire Thomas or ABA sites to PDF would be time consuming, bandwidth intensive, and produce a monstrously huge file).

Working with PDF Files

5

Think of working with PDF documents as working with a notebook full of paper documents. Just as with a notebook or file folder full of paper, you can add pages to PDF files (at the point of your choosing), remove pages (take them out, copy, and reinsert), and delete pages (take them out and discard) from PDF files. Beyond the basics of taking pages in and out, you can build an electronic table of contents using bookmarks and create links (you can build a link from virtually any point within a PDF files to lots of other types of digital information, not just other PDF files). Another aspect of working with PDF files involves settings that control how you want your PDF file to look when you or someone else opens it, including how the pages are numbered. When you set the look of your PDF file, you can also build in some identifying features so that your document can be found using Windows Explorer or other search software in case it ends up in the wrong place in your filing system.

From the very first day that you were a lawyer, you have probably worked with paper documents collected in file folders, notebooks, boxes, and various other means of keeping certain pages together and other pages apart. Whether the pages were client files organized in folders or notebooks, or boxes full of paper produced in discovery, you have basically dealt with paper. Paper documents consist of pages that can be organized in a myriad of ways. PDF files consist of pages, and like their paper counterparts, the pages can be organized in any number of ways. Sometimes the pages that exist as paper in a folder, notebook, or box are collected together as a single PDF file. Other times, those pages might be split into multiple files and may even be stored in various electronic file folders (directories). As you read the material in this chapter, think initially in terms of one large document such as a thousand pages of discovery or a hundred-page contract. That will provide a good mental framework for seeing the similarity between working with paper and working with PDF files.

The material in Chapter 16, "Acrobat in the Paperless Office," provides more information on working with and organizing large collections (such as all the files in your office). There you will learn some basic file-naming conventions and folder-organization tips that make working with multiple PDF documents seem, again, much like working with paper documents. For now, we'll focus on what you can do with a single multipage PDF document.

§ 5.1 Add Pages

Okay, you have a PDF file—whether one page or a thousand-plus pages—and you want to add more pages. New pages can be inserted at any point in the PDF file; you need only decide whether the page or pages are added before or after the insertion point. For example, in a ten-page document you need to add three new pages between the current pages 7 and 8. If you open the existing file and turn to page 7, then you would insert the new pages after the insertion point; if you were at page 8, the insertion would be before. The pages to be added, or inserted, can be single-page or multiple-page PDF documents. To add pages:

  6.0 Menu (Add Pages): **Document** > **Pages** > **Insert**
  7.0 Menu (Add Pages): **Document** > **Insert Pages**
  Keystroke (Add Pages): **Shift**+**Ctrl**+**I**

See Figure 5.1 below.

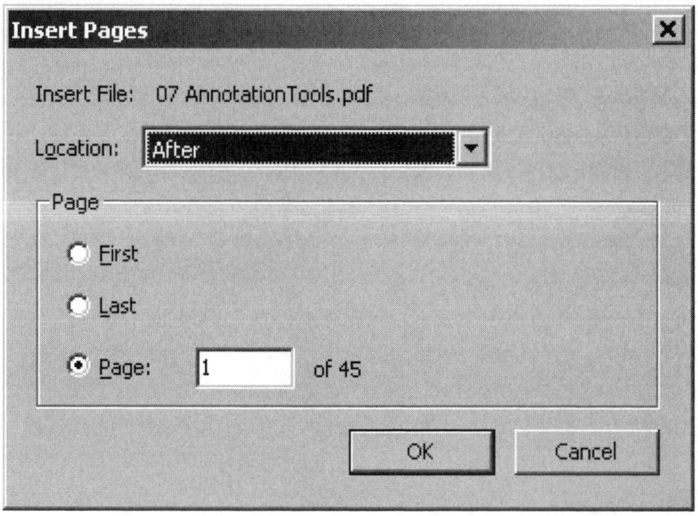

Figure 5.1

§ 5.2 Extract Pages

Extracting pages means taking pages out of a PDF document and saving them as a separate document (they may continue to exist as a separate document or may be inserted into another document or documents). To extract pages:

6.0 Menu Command (Extract Pages): **Document** > **Pages** > **Extract**
7.0 Menu Command (Extract Pages): **Document** > **Extract Pages**
6.0 Keystroke (Extract Pages): **Alt+D-P-E**
7.0 Keystroke (Extract Pages): **Alt+D-X**

Extracting pages from a PDF document is equivalent to taking paper pages out of a folder, notebook, or box, making copies, and then putting the pages right back where they came from. The paper copies are the extracted pages. You can work with these pages, save them, or throw them away. For example, if you have a fifty-page contract and you only want to use page 3 (containing a legal description of real property) as an exhibit, then you would extract page 3 and save the extracted page with a new name (such as "001 Exhibit 1 LegalDescription.pdf"). The original fifty-page contract would not be altered in any way (there is no risk that you have put page 3 back in the wrong place).

When you extract pages, the **Extract Pages** dialog box appears (Figure 5.2).

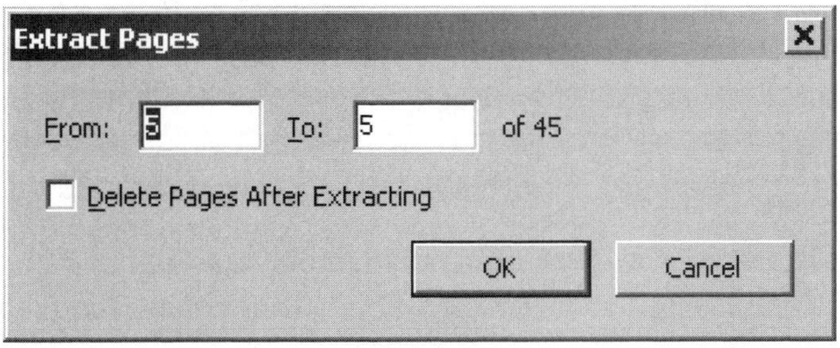

Figure 5.2

Notice the checkbox option that allows you to **Delete Pages After Extracting.** When you extract pages, the extracted pages appear in a new window. If the box is checked, the extracted pages are no longer in the original document—they have been deleted. The extracted pages that appear in the new window must be saved with a new file name if you want to keep them. Extracting pages with the **Delete Pages After Extracting** box checked is useful when reviewing a document for privileged material. As you go through the document you extract (and delete) the privileged pages; the extracted pages are then named and saved in a manner that reflects their privileged status. The original document exists, but without the privileged material.

§ 5.3 Delete Pages

Deleting takes the pages out of the current PDF document and throws them away. No, they do not go to the recycle bin so that you can retrieve them if you change your mind! This is taking pages out of a notebook and running them through the shredder; they are gone for good (so use with caution). This feature is handy for ripping out blank pages. To delete pages:

> 6.0 Menu (Delete Pages): **Document** > **Pages** > **Delete**
> 7.0 Menu (Delete Pages): **Document** > **Delete Pages**
> Keystroke (Delete Pages): **Ctrl+Shift+D**

Notice that once you have told Acrobat to delete a page, the **Delete Pages** dialog box appears. (See Figure 5.3). If you want to delete only the current page, tap the **Enter** key (or click on **OK**), and it is gone (for good). If you want to delete a series of consecutive pages, specify the range in the **Delete Pages** dialog box. Notice that the current page is by default selected as the beginning point for the From-To range.

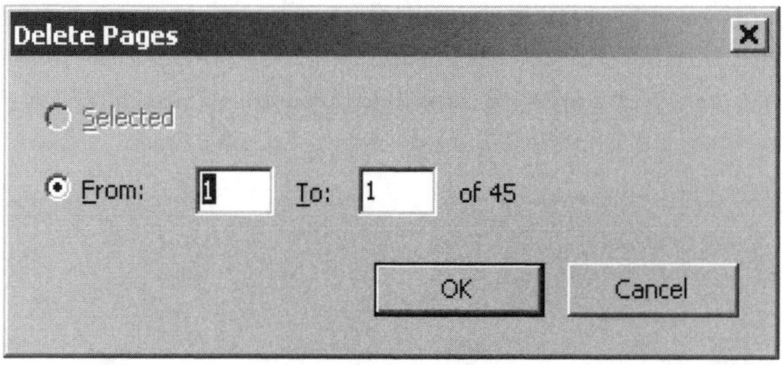

Figure 5.3

Use **Delete Pages** with caution. Remember, this is not removing pages and putting them in the trash or recycle bin (from where you might get them back if you're lucky).

§ 5.4 Crop Pages

Sometimes the information on a page can be enhanced by removing extraneous materials from the edges (you know, those black borders from the photocopy process). This is also handy when someone scans in a bunch of pages to legal size when they should have been letter size. If you use Acrobat in display mode, **Crop Pages** can be used to carve out a portion of a document so that it can be displayed following a full-page display to create an effective zoom effect. (See Figures 5.4 and 5.5.)

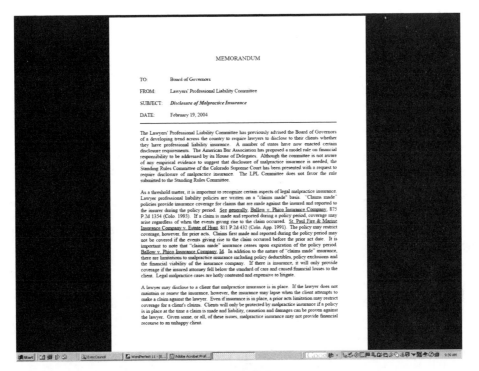

Figure 5.4

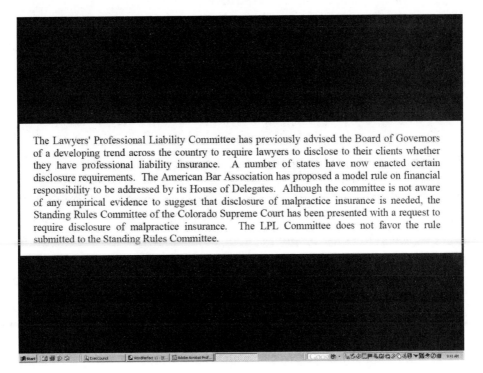

The Lawyers' Professional Liability Committee has previously advised the Board of Governors of a developing trend across the country to require lawyers to disclose to their clients whether they have professional liability insurance. A number of states have now enacted certain disclosure requirements. The American Bar Association has proposed a model rule on financial responsibility to be addressed by its House of Delegates. Although the committee is not aware of any empirical evidence to suggest that disclosure of malpractice insurance is needed, the Standing Rules Committee of the Colorado Supreme Court has been presented with a request to require disclosure of malpractice insurance. The LPL Committee does not favor the rule submitted to the Standing Rules Committee.

Figure 5.5

To crop pages:

> 6.0 Menu (Crop Pages): **Document** > **Pages** > **Crop**
> 7.0 Menu (Crop Pages): **Document** > **Crop Pages**
> Keystroke (Crop Pages): **Shift+Ctrl+T**

Once the menu or keyboard commands have been issued, a dialog box appears allowing the user to set the parameters for cropping. The current page, all pages, or a range of pages can be cropped.

§ 5.5 Rotate Pages

Now this is something you cannot do in your paper notebook, or at least not with as good a result. You will find it particularly useful with scanned documents; by virtue of mechanics all documents go through the scanner in portrait orientation regardless of how the information was set on the physical page. It is also handy when someone places the pages in the scanner top down, so that the resulting images are upside down. To rotate single or multiple pages to correct the orientation:

> 6.0 Menu (Rotate Pages): **Document** > **Pages** > **Rotate**
> 7.0 Menu (Rotate Pages): **Document** > **Rotate Pages**
> Keystroke (Rotate Pages): **Ctrl+Shift+R**

Once the menu or keyboard commands have been issued, a dialog box appears allowing you to set the parameters for rotating pages, including the direction and amount of rotation (clockwise 90 degrees, counter-clockwise 90 degrees, or 180 degrees). (See Figure 5.6). The current page, all pages, or a range of pages can be rotated. Note: Rotate View (**View** > **Rotate View**) is different; that function rotates the view for the entire document and cannot be saved.

§ 5.6 Rearranging Page Order Using the Thumbnail View

You have added, extracted, deleted, cropped, and rotated pages—and now you want page 5 to come before page 3. To accomplish this, use the Thumbnail view to drag and drop pages to reorder them. To rearrange pages using thumbnails:

1. Select the **Pages** tab on the navigation pane.
2. Left-click on the desired page, and while holding down the left button, drag the page to the desired location; multiple pages can be selected by holding down the **Ctrl** key while then clicking on the desired pages. (See Figure 5.7).

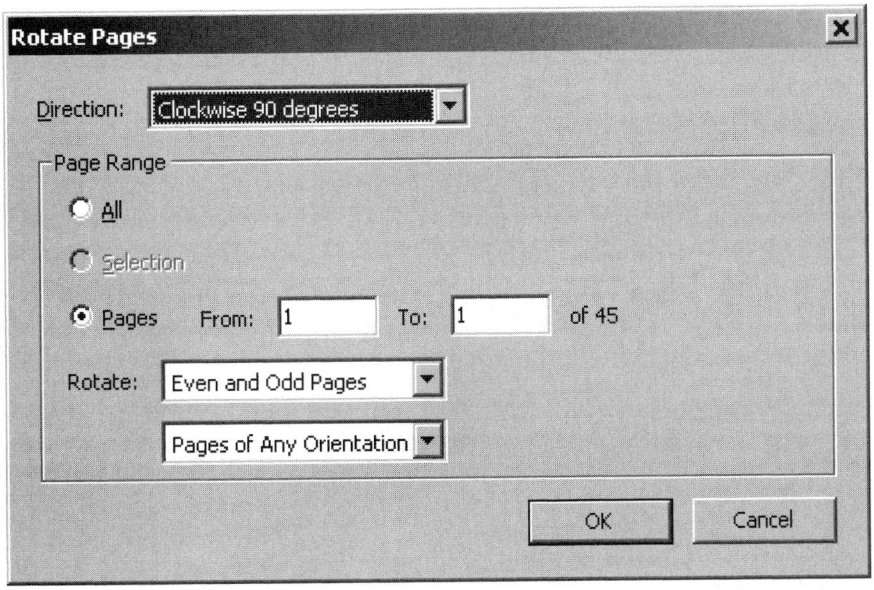

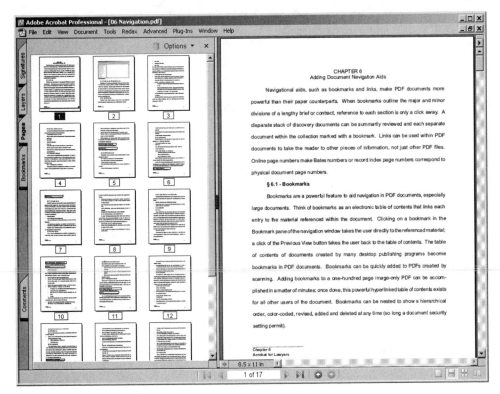

Figure 5.6

Figure 5.7

3. As the page or pages are moved by dragging, a vertical bar appears between the thumbnails displayed in the Pages window; when the desired destination has been reached simply release the left button on the mouse (pointer).

This feature works well for small documents, but the larger the document, the less practical it becomes (it's pretty hard to drag page 499 to the page 3 position). If faced with this situation, consider extracting the page or pages to be moved (with the **Delete Pages After Extracting** option checked; see the discussion in section 5.2 above), then reinserting them (see section 5.1).

§ 5.7 Document Open Options

The way a PDF file appears on the display when opened can be controlled by setting initial view in the **Document Properties** window (See Figure 5.8, Version 6.0; for Version 7.0, see Figure 5.9).

If bookmarks have been created, then you may want anyone who opens the document to see, in the initial view, the **Bookmarks** tab in the navigation

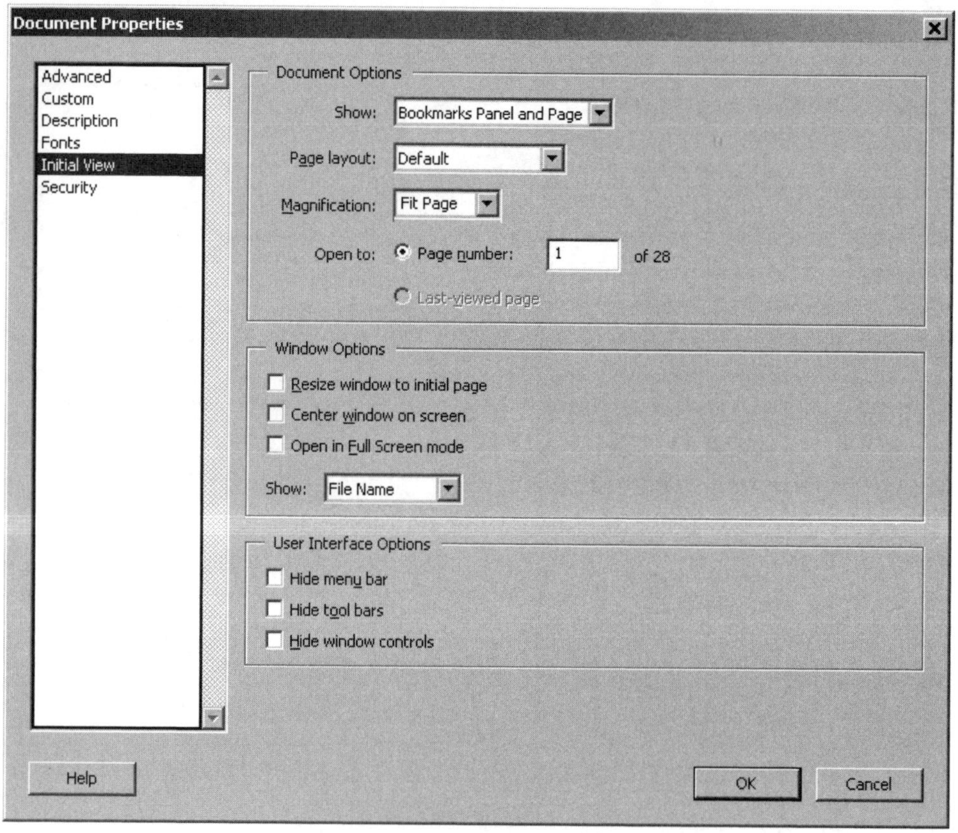

Figure 5.8

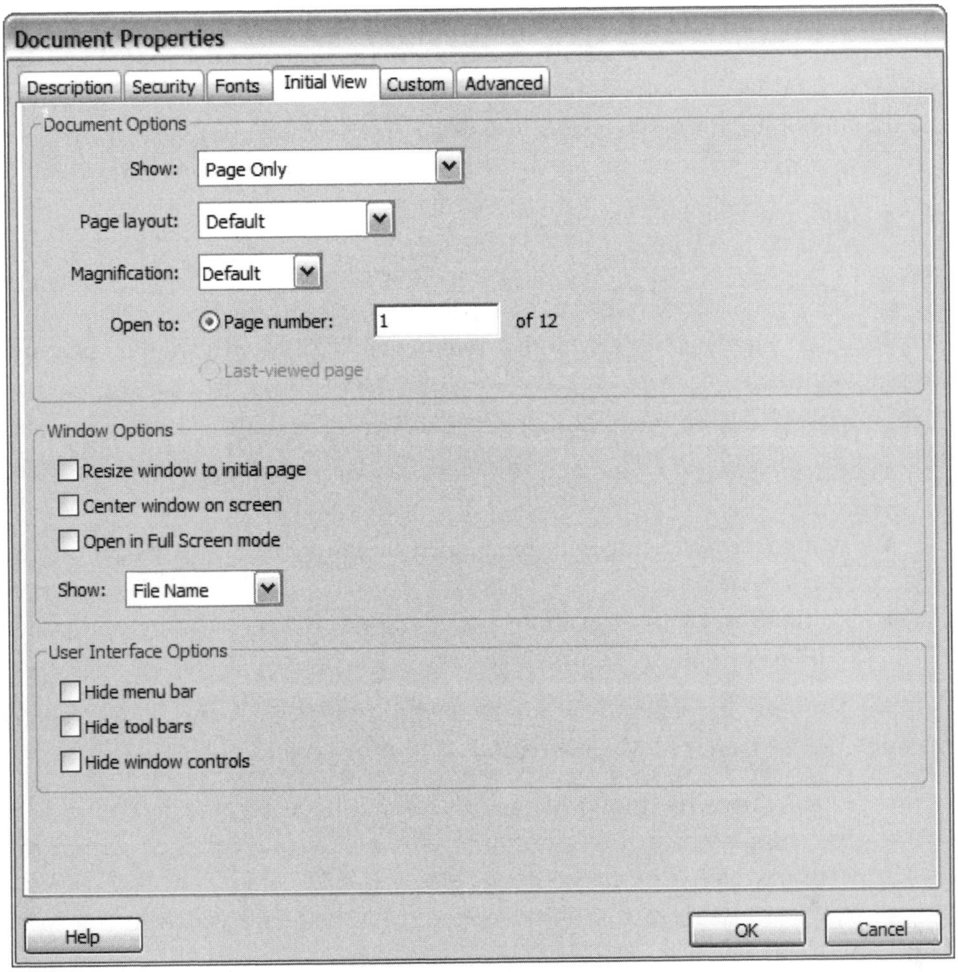

Figure 5.9

window. For example, when sending a lengthy document to a client for review, or submitting an electronic brief that contains various sections and exhibits, it helps to show the client or court that the document contains bookmarks. With a few clicks of the mouse and using the **Document Properties** window, you can establish how the document appears when others open it. To access the **Document Properties** window:

Menu (Document Properties Window Initial View): **File** > **Document Properties** (select **Initial View** in the left pane Version 6.0; select **Initial View tab** Version 7.0)

Keystroke (Document Properties Window Initial View): **Ctrl+D** (select **Initial View** in the left pane Version 6.0; select **Initial View tab** Version 7.0)

Once the menu or keyboard commands have been issued and **Initial View** has been selected in the left pane or by clicking on the Initial View tab, options for how the document appears upon opening can be selected (Figure 5.4). The top section (**Document Options**) of the **Document Properties—Initial View** window contains the most salient features. First, you can select how the document appears with the **Show** drop-down menu:

- ◆ Page Only
- ◆ Bookmarks Panel and Page
- ◆ Pages Panel and Page
- ◆ Layers Panel and Page

Next, you can specify how individual pages display with the **Page Layout** drop-down menu:

- ◆ Default (uses the individual user's default page display settings)
- ◆ Single Page (one page at a time appears on the screen)
- ◆ Continuous (pages scroll from one to the next)
- ◆ Facing (multiple pages appear on the display and navigation occurs one page at a time)
- ◆ Continuous Facing (multiple pages appear on the display and pages scroll from one to the next)

Next, you can specify how much of the display area the pages use by making choices from the **Magnification** drop-down menu:

- ◆ Default (uses the individual user's default page display settings)
- ◆ Percentage views (the document is magnified or reduced within the display area by the percentage selected)
- ◆ Fit Page (displays the entire page, full height and width in the work area)
- ◆ Fit Width (displays the page in full width; generally requires scrolling to see the bottom portion of each page but provides for a larger image)
- ◆ Fit Visible (provides a slightly wider view than Fit Width)

§ 5.8 Document Summary

Think of PDF Document Summaries as card catalog entries. Having card catalog entries for image-only PDF documents can make a world of difference in locating documents using the search function in Windows Explorer or other file searching tools. Remember, image-only PDFs are just that—images only, just digital photocopies of paper documents. Without document summaries, the location of a given image-only PDF file can be determined only by knowing its file name. Searching for the file by name can be narrowed down a bit using other criteria such as date range and file type. But in the end, finding image-only files by file name comes down to a manual search, just like rifling through a box of paper looking for a particular document. If an image-only file happens to be saved to the wrong folder (accidents do happen), the manual search to find it can be time-consuming and problematic.

The perils of a manual search can be avoided by using Document Summaries. With Document Summaries the power of the computer can be harnessed to locate specific information. Information contained in the Document Summary can be found by Windows Explorer searches of files and folders containing certain text. To create a document summary:

Menu (Document Summary): **File** > **Document Properties** (select **Description** in the left pane Version 6.0; select the **Description** tab Version 7.0)

Keystroke (Document Summary): **Ctrl+D** (select **Description** in the left pane Version 6.0; select the **Description** tab Version 7.0)

Once the menu or keyboard commands have been issued, and **Description** selected in the left pane of the **Document Properties** window (Version 6.0) or the **Description** tab selected (Version 7.0), a dialog box appears for entering information to be contained in the Document Summary. (See Figure 5.10, Version 6.0). Text entered in any of the four fields (Title, Author, Subject,

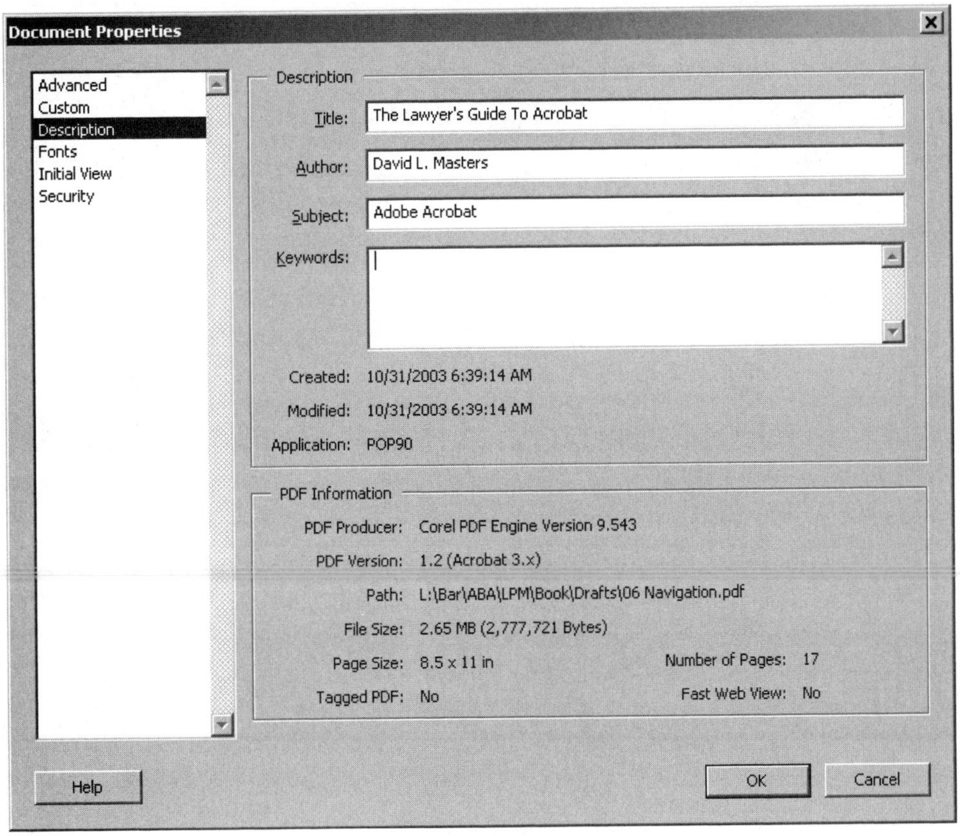

Figure 5.10

and Keywords) can be found using a Windows Explorer search for files containing the specified text. In Version 7.0, the **Description** tab display in the **Document Properties** window looks slightly different and allows for the input of **Additional MetaData.** See Figures 5.11 and 5.12.

Document summaries are meta data. So, depending on what you include in the document summary, you may want to edit or delete the contents of the Document Summary before sharing the PDF file with others (such as electronic court filings and discovery responses).

§ 5.9 Chapter 5 Wrap-up

If you read this chapter from start to finish, congratulations—it contains a lot of important information. Please don't think that you need to commit the in-

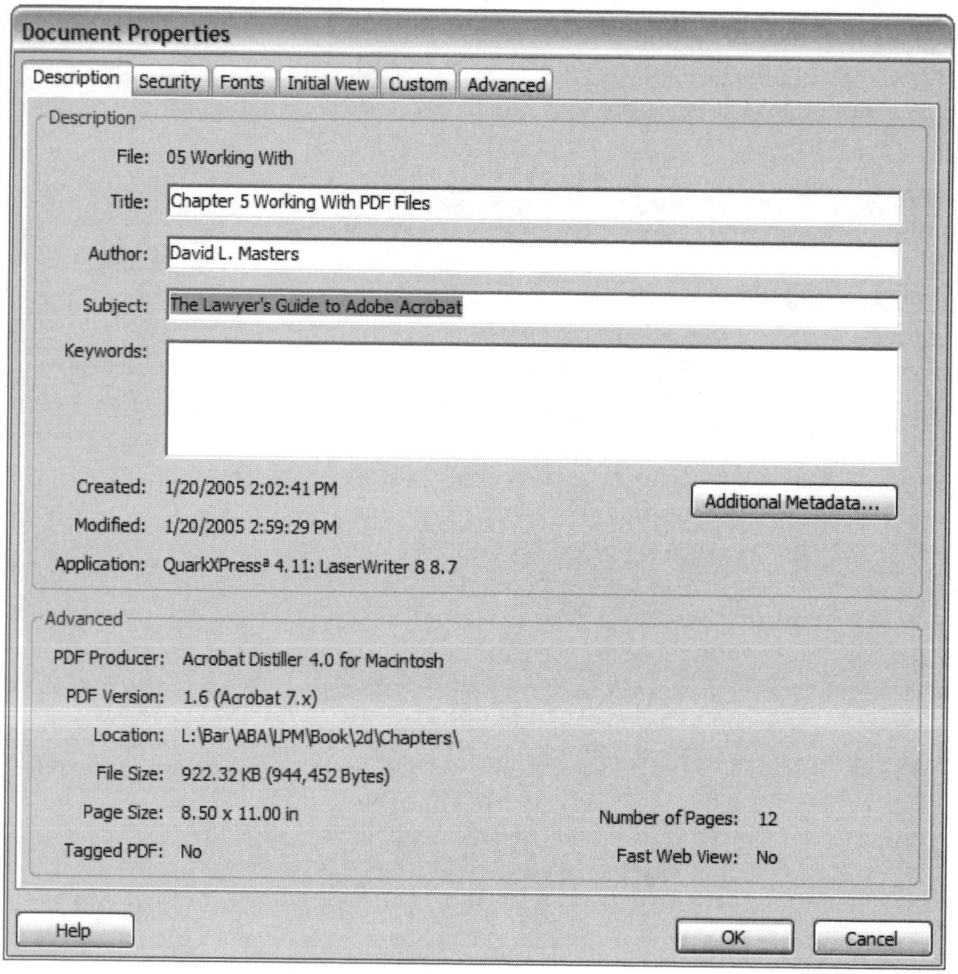

Figure 5.11

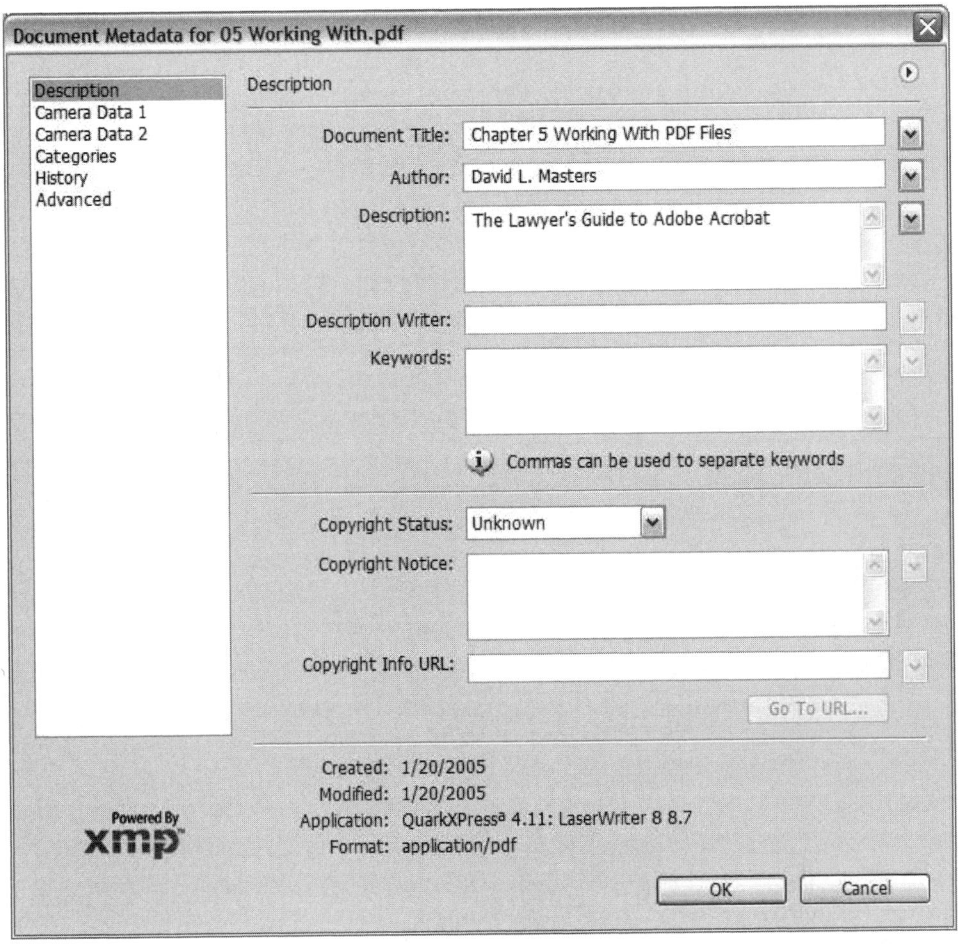

Figure 5.12

formation to memory. Instead, make a test copy of a medium-sized document (fifty to five hundred pages) and spend an hour adding, extracting, deleting, rotating, cropping, and moving pages. After an hour, working with PDF files will be second nature to you.

Adding Document Navigation Aids

6

Navigation aids, such as bookmarks and links, make PDF files more powerful than their paper counterparts. When bookmarks outline the major and minor divisions of a lengthy brief or contract, reference to each section is only a click away. A disparate stack of discovery documents can be quickly reviewed and each separate document within the collection marked with a bookmark. Bookmarks are the quick way to organize and provide navigation in PDF files (Figure 6.1).

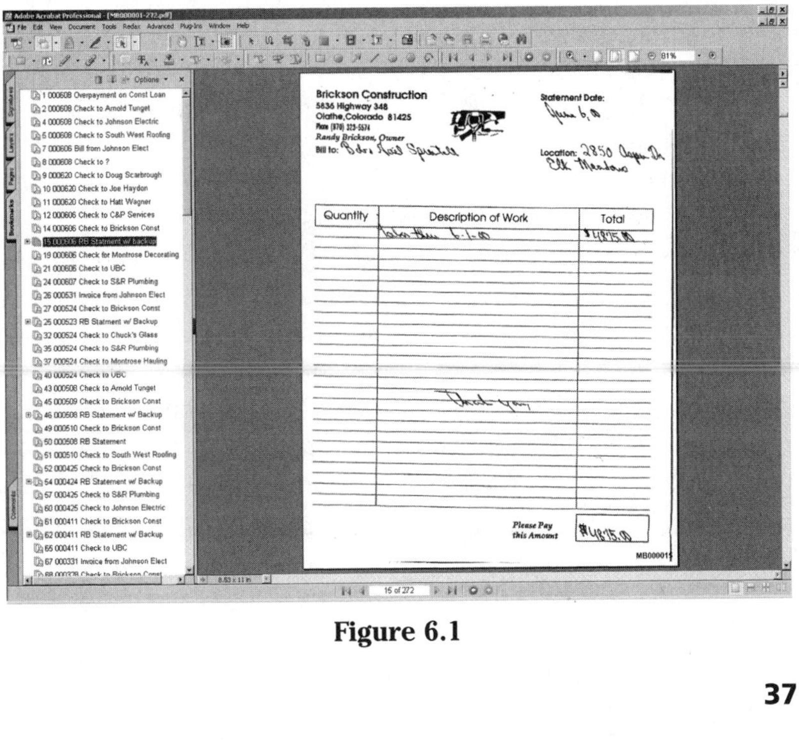

Figure 6.1

Think of bookmarks as an easily created hyperlinked table of contents. Links are similar to bookmarks in that they can take you, or any other viewer of a PDF file, from point A to point B with a click of the mouse. Unlike bookmarks, which appear in the navigation pane external to the document, links exist internally within documents. Links within PDF files are much like links within Web pages—click here (on the link) and go to a different page. Links can be used within PDF files to take the reader to other pieces of information, not just to other PDF files. Online or virtual page numbers make Bates numbers or record index page numbers correspond to physical document page numbers, thus enabling the reader to navigate by using the **Go To Page** *n* function.

§ 6.1 Bookmarks

Bookmarks are a powerful feature to aid navigation in PDF documents, especially large documents. For little effort, bookmarks produce big returns in document organization and navigation. Again, think of bookmarks as an electronic table of contents that links each entry to the material referenced within the document. Clicking on a bookmark in the Bookmarks pane of the navigation window takes you directly to the referenced material. The table-of-contents elements created by some desktop publishing programs become bookmarks when those documents are printed (converted) to PDF. Bookmarks can be quickly added to image-only PDFs created by scanning. Adding bookmarks to a one-hundred-page image-only PDF can be accomplished in a matter of minutes; once done, this powerful hyperlinked table of contents exists for all other users of the document. Bookmarks can be nested to show a hierarchical order, color coded, revised, added, and deleted at any time (as long as document security settings permit).

§ 6.1.1 Using Bookmarks with Litigation Documents

Bookmarks can be used to organize and navigate document collections produced in litigation. For example, opposing counsel has delivered five hundred pages of medical records. These pages can be scanned to a single PDF file and bookmarks added. The bookmarks could be one for each discrete record, or grouped by treating physician. The initial review and bookmarking can be performed by staff or by a lawyer. This first quick trip through the documents to add bookmarks provides an opportunity for the lawyer to make a preliminary assessment of the content, and adding bookmarks provides a lasting organizational scheme to quickly navigate within the document.

While bookmarks look and act like a hyperlinked table of contents (a linear depiction of subject matter within a document), with a little imagination they can be used in a nonlinear fashion and consequently put to a slightly different purpose. Rather than creating bookmarks that describe the referenced materials linearly by subject, consider creating a set of bookmarks that reflect issues (liability, damages, and so on). (See Figure 6.2.)

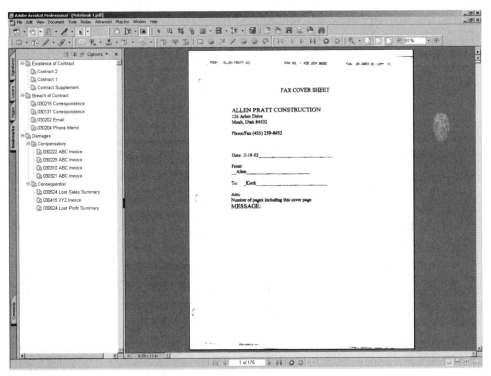

Figure 6.2

The issue bookmarks would be the primary level of a bookmark hierarchy, with nested marks using content- or subject-descriptive titles to link each portion of a document to an issue. This arrangement would be nonlinear insofar as the issues need not be listed in the order of appearance within a document; the nested marks might even be coded and ranked by the power or weight with which the referenced material supports the parent issue.

§ 6.1.2 Creating Bookmarks

Bookmarks can be created in a variety of ways, some more complicated than others. The preferred method is the simplest. To quickly create a bookmark:

1. Press **Ctrl+B.**
2. Type a short description.
3. Press **Enter.**

The simple command (**Ctrl+B**) opens the Bookmarks tab on the navigation pane and adds a blank bookmark to the end of the list; typing a short description names the bookmark, and pressing the **Enter** key completes the process. If you prefer working with the Acrobat user interface, to create a bookmark do the following:

1. Click the **Bookmarks** tab in the navigation pane.
2. Click the bookmark after which you want to place the new bookmark. If you don't select a bookmark, the new bookmark is automatically added at the end of the list.
3. Choose **New Bookmark** from the **Options** menu in the navigation pane.
4. Select the new bookmark and do *one* of the following:
   a) Choose **View** > **Toolbars** > **Properties,** and choose a color and style for the text
   b) Right-click and select **Properties.** Click the **Appearance** tab, and choose a color and style for the text; you can open the **Bookmark Properties** dialog box by clicking the **More** button on the **Properties** toolbar
5. On the **Bookmarks** tab, select the **Untitled** label of the new bookmark and type the text you want.

After you have defined a bookmark's appearance, you can reuse the appearance settings by selecting the bookmark, right-clicking, and choosing **Use Current Appearance as New Default.**

§ 6.1.3 Bookmarking Selected Text or Image

In image-on-text PDF files, bookmarks can be targeted to specific text or graphics. Remember, image-on-text files are created by printing text-based documents to PDF or processing image-only files with an OCR application. Bookmarks that link to selected text can be particularly useful to direct readers to specific passages within a document. For example, you might print a case to PDF and highlight a section that you want the court or opposing counsel to focus on. A bookmark linked to the selected text would take the reader to the highlighted passage.

Bookmarks to selected text take the reader directly to the referenced information. Recall that Acrobat has three standard page views: Actual Size, Fit Page, and Fit Width. When documents are displayed in the Actual Size or Fit Width view, only a portion of the current page appears in the work area. If you create a bookmark that links to a page and the information that you want the reader to see happens to be at the bottom of the page, the relationship may not be apparent. However, if you create a bookmark by selecting text, then clicking on the mark takes the reader to the exact location in the document where the text appears, and the relationship is apparent. Consider using Select Text to create bookmarks that correspond to headings in a contract, brief, or other long image-on-text PDF files.

To create a bookmark that targets specific text:

1. Click on the **Select Text** tool on the toolbar.
2. Select the text (the selected text becomes the label of the new bookmark; you can edit the label).
3. Press **Ctrl+B.**
4. Press **Enter.**

If you prefer working with the Acrobat user interface, to create a bookmark do the following:

Select the **Select Text** tool on the toolbar and do *one* of the following:
   a) Drag to select the text (the selected text becomes the label of the new bookmark; you can edit the label)
   b) Right-click and choose **Add Bookmark**

A process similar to that described above for creating bookmarks using the Select Text tool can used for creating bookmarks that are linked to specific graphics or portions of graphics. The Select Graphic tool is used in place of the Select Text tool and the bookmark label must be typed (the graphic or portion of a graphic selected does not supply the bookmark label).

§ 6.1.4 Changing Bookmark Appearance

The appearance of bookmarks, including the name, font, and color, can be changed at any time. You may want to change the appearance of certain bookmarks for various reasons. For example, changes in appearance can be used to signify importance or to do issue coding. Using color to differentiate bookmarks (even a set of basic linear bookmarks—the table of contents) can produce rudimentary issue coding.

To change a bookmark's name or appearance, do *one* of the following:

a) Select the bookmark in the **Bookmarks** tab, choose **Rename Bookmark** in the **Options** menu, and type the new bookmark name
b) Select the bookmark in the **Bookmarks** tab, right-click, and choose **Rename**
c) Select the bookmark, right-click, and select **Properties**; in the **Appearance** tab, change the color and style of the text

Bookmark appearance and action can also be set using the **Bookmark Properties** dialog box (see Figures 6.3 and 6.4). To set the appearance or action of a bookmark using the **Bookmark Properties** dialog box, first click on the bookmark to be altered, then:

Menu (Bookmark Properties Bar Select): **View** > **Toolbars** > **Properties Bar**
Keystroke (Bookmark Properties Bar Select): **Ctrl+E** or **Alt+V-T-P**

Bookmark Properties

Appearance | Actions

Style: Plain ▼

Color:

Close

Figure 6.3

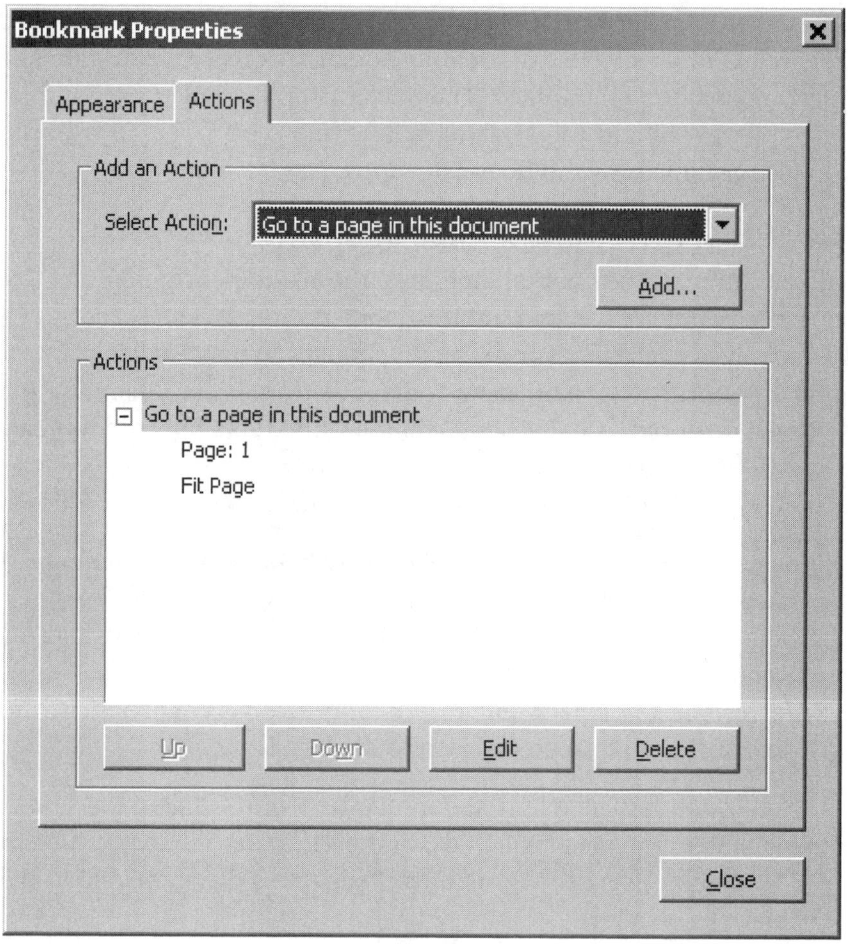

Bookmark Properties

Appearance | Actions

Add an Action

Select Action: Go to a page in this document ▼

Add...

Actions

⊟ Go to a page in this document
        Page: 1
        Fit Page

Up | Down | Edit | Delete

Close

Figure 6.4

§ 6.1.5 Editing the Bookmark Destination

The destination or target of a bookmark can be changed at any time. To edit the destination of a bookmark:

1. Go to the page in the document that will be the new destination.
2. Right-click on the bookmark to edit and select **Set Destination**; a warning that you are about to make a change appears (see Figure 6.5).

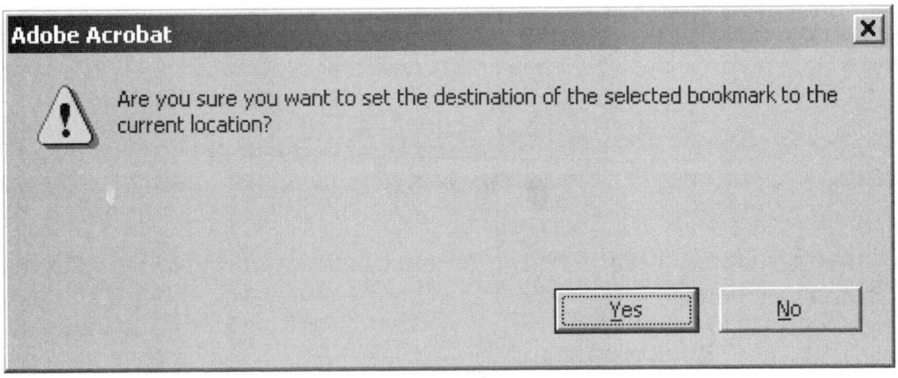

Figure 6.5

3. Click **Yes** to confirm the change of address.

If you prefer working with the Acrobat user interface, to change the destination of a bookmark do the following:

1. Click the **Bookmarks** tab and select the bookmark.
2. In the document pane, move to the location you want to specify as the new destination.
3. Choose **Set Bookmark Destination** in the **Options** menu or right-click and select **Set Destination.**
4. Click **Yes** to confirm the change of address.

§ 6.1.6 Deleting Bookmarks

Bookmarks, being the powerful and flexible tool they are, can be removed from documents at will. To delete a single bookmark:

1. Right-click on the bookmark to be removed.
2. Select **Delete.**

To delete multiple bookmarks:

1. Hold down the **Control (Ctrl)** key and click on the bookmarks to be removed.
2. Select **Delete**.

See Figure 6.6 below.

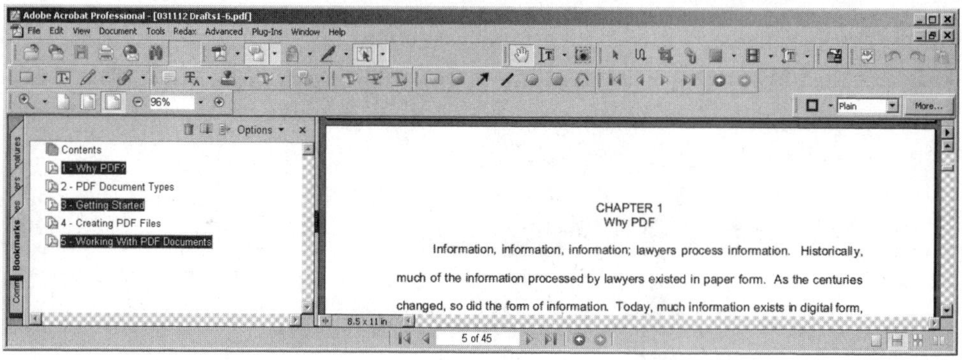

Figure 6.6

If you prefer working with the Acrobat user interface, to delete a bookmark do the following:

1. Click the **Bookmarks** tab.
2. Select the bookmark and do *one* of the following:
    a) Choose **Delete Bookmark** in the **Options** menu
    b) Right-click and choose **Delete**
    c) Drag the bookmarks to the trash can

Caution: Deleting a bookmark deletes any bookmarks that are subordinate to it. Deleting a bookmark does not delete any document text.

Caution: Unlike changing the destination, you are not given an opportunity to confirm the deletion; when you select **Delete,** the bookmark disappears. Inadvertent deletions can be recovered immediately using the Undo command.

To undo the deletion of a bookmark:

Menu (Undo Delete Bookmark): **Edit** > **Undo Delete Bookmark**
Keystroke (Undo Delete Bookmark): **Ctrl+Z** or **Alt+E-U**

The Undo command can be executed a number of times to undo a series of actions, including the deletion of bookmarks. The Acrobat Help manual does not indicate how many levels of undo are available.

§ 6.1.7 Wrapping Long Bookmarks

Sometimes the name you give to a bookmark is just too long to be displayed in the Bookmarks tab of the navigation pane. There are several ways to deal with this problem. First, rename the bookmark with a shorter name. If shortening the name is not an option, then the navigation pane can be resized to display more text; however, this option correspondingly decreases the size of the document window. If long bookmark names are a necessity, then the elegant solution is to wrap the text in the bookmark name (see Figure 6.7).

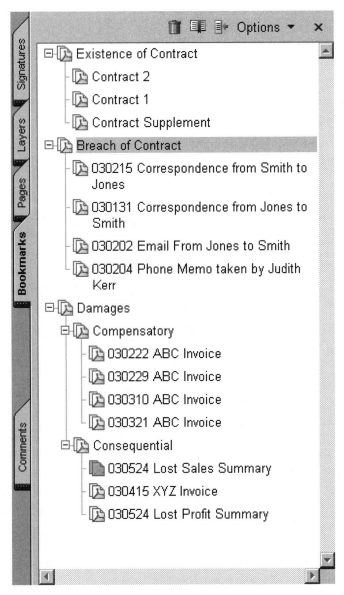

Figure 6.7

To wrap the text in long bookmarks:

1. Select any bookmark.
2. Right-click and select **Wrap Long Bookmarks**.

If you prefer working with the Acrobat user interface, to wrap the text in long bookmarks do the following:

> In the Bookmarks tab, choose **Wrap Long Bookmarks** from the **Options** menu to show all the text of long bookmarks regardless of the width of the Bookmarks tab.

Regardless of the method used to wrap the text in long bookmarks, this option is on when checked and off when not checked.

§ 6.1.8 Bookmark Hierarchy

You can nest a list of bookmarks to show a relationship between destinations or topics. Nesting creates a parent-child relationship. You can expand and collapse this hierarchical list as desired (see Figure 6.8).

To expand and collapse the bookmark hierarchy, do *one* of the following:

a) Click the plus sign or horizontal triangle next to the bookmark icon to show any children related to the bookmark; click the minus sign or inverted triangle to collapse the list again

b) Select the bookmark, and choose **Expand Current Bookmark** from the **Options** menu

c) From the **Options** menu, choose **Expand Top-Level Bookmarks** to show all bookmarks

d) Choose **Collapse Top-Level Bookmarks** to collapse all bookmarks

§ 6.1.8.1 Nesting a Bookmark Under Another Bookmark

To create a hierarchy after bookmarks have been created, it is necessary to move individual bookmarks or groups of bookmarks up or down (in and out) in the hierarchy. Moving a bookmark to a lower level in the hierarchy is accomplished by nesting. To nest a bookmark or group of bookmarks under another bookmark, do the following:

1. Select the bookmark or range of bookmarks to be nested.
2. Drag the icon or icons directly underneath the parent bookmark icon (a line shows the position of the icon or icons).
3. Release the bookmark and nesting is complete (the destination remains in its original location).

§ 6.1.8.2 Moving a Bookmark Out of a Nested Position

Just as bookmarks can be nested to create a hierarchy, so can they be "unnested" or moved out of nested position when necessary. To move a bookmark out of a nested position:

1. Select the bookmark or range of bookmarks to be moved.
2. Drag the icon or icons in an upward direction to position the small arrow directly under the label of the parent bookmark.
3. Release the bookmark.

§ 6.1.9 Bookmark Security

Now that you know how easy it is to change bookmark properties (name, destination, and so on), maybe you don't want other users to change your book-

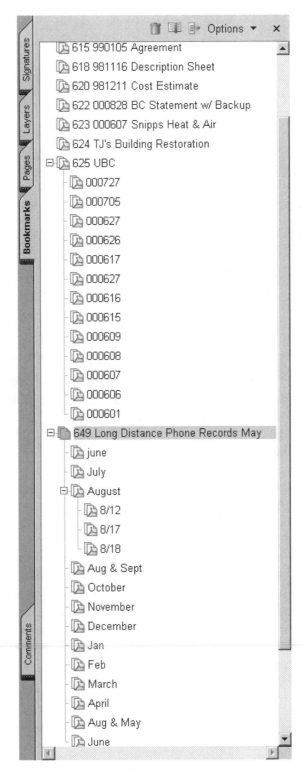

Figure 6.8

marks. Basic PDF file security can be used to restrict the ability of others to make changes (Figure 6.9).

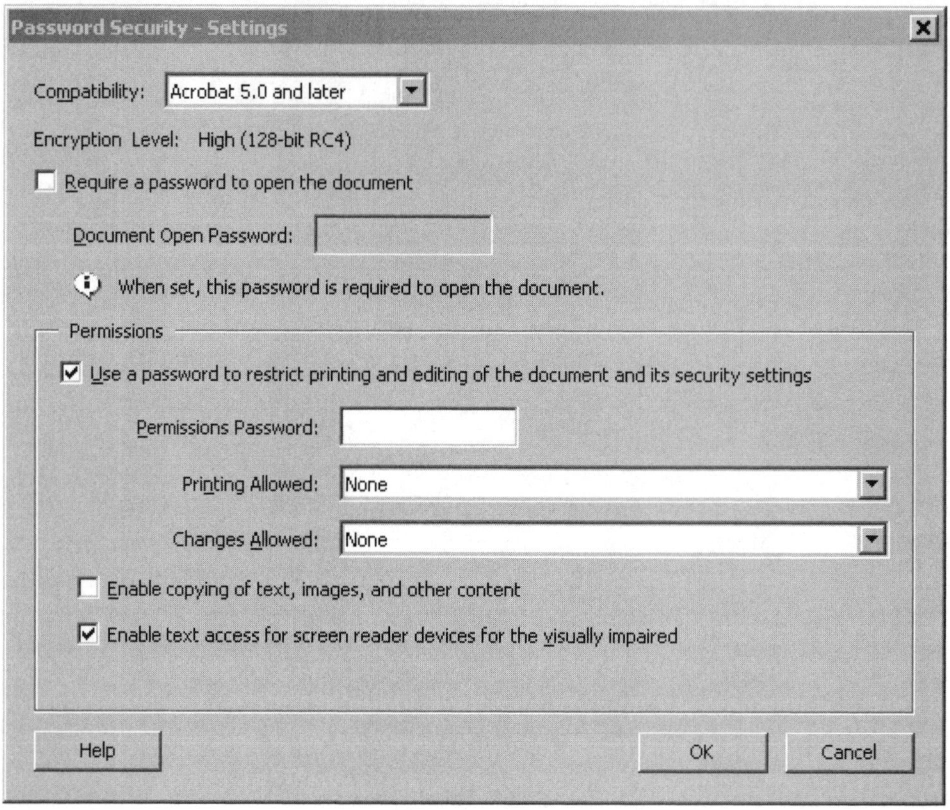

Figure 6.9

In the **Password Security—Settings** dialog box, setting **Changes Allowed** (in the **Permissions** section) to **None** requires other users to enter the correct password before bookmark properties can be changed. Basic **Password Security** looks and functions a bit differently in Version 7.0. It's still in the **Document Properties** window, but is selected by clicking on the **Security** tab (see Figure 6.10). From this point, select the type of security desired from the drop-down menu (**No Security, Password Security, Certificate Security,** or **Adobe Policy Server**). If you select **Password Security**, the next dialog box will look like Figure 6.11. Select the desired security settings and click OK.

§ 6.2 Links

Links make PDF documents interactive and truly powerful. In the transactional practice, think of a long contract with links built into it that take the reader to the various exhibits or schedules to the contract. Every reference

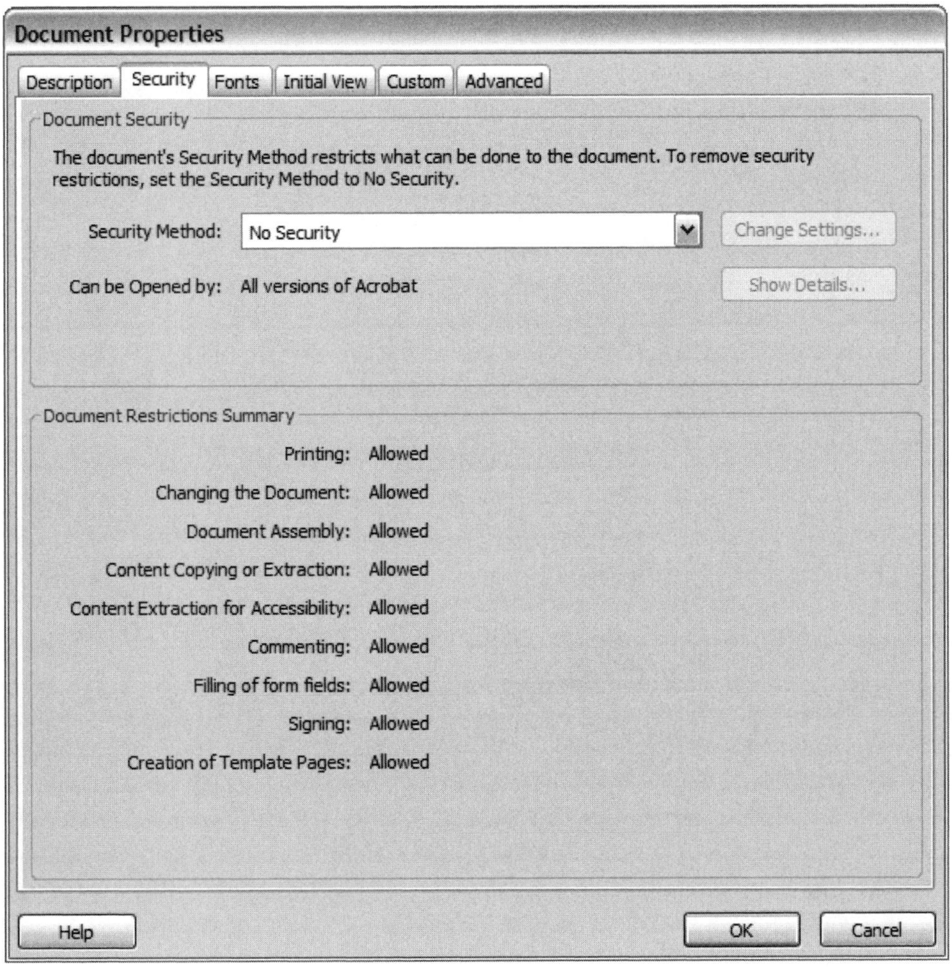

Figure 6.10

to Exhibit A can be linked to that exhibit; a click on the link takes the reader to the exhibit. (**Tip:** Remember, the best way back to the point of the link is the Previous View button at the bottom of the work area.) In the litigation context, links are the magic that add power to electronic briefs. When a citation to a case, statute, or other authority appears in your brief, it can be linked to the cited material so that with a click of the mouse the reader sees the authority you have cited. Links let you and other readers of the document jump to other locations in the same document, to other electronic documents, to Web sites, and more. Links can initiate actions, such as playing a sound or movie file. They can be visible or invisible (color-coded invisible links are the best).

Of the commonly used power features of Acrobat, links are probably the most difficult to master. That said, once mastered, links bring a level of interactivity to PDF files that simply cannot be matched in the paper world.

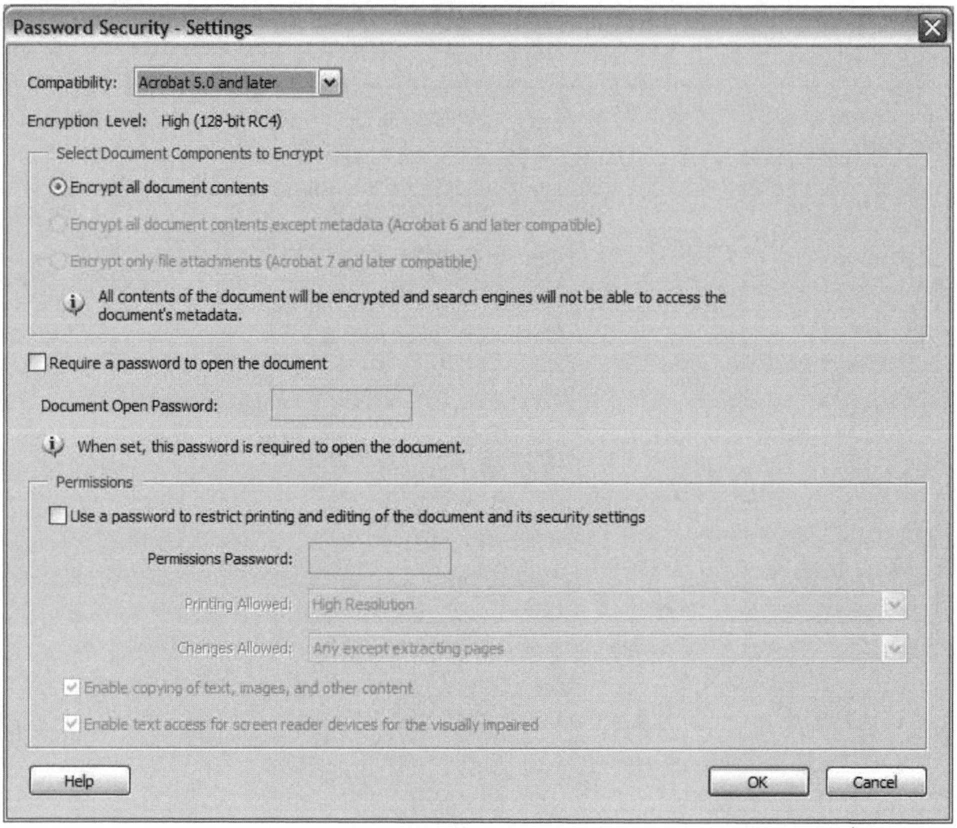

Figure 6.11

§ 6.2.1 The Link Tool

Links are created in PDF documents using the Link tool. The Link tool looks like two links of connected chain (Figure 6.12); it resides on the Advanced Editing toolbar, so before you can use it you must display that toolbar.

Figure 6.12

To display the Advanced Editing toolbar:

Menu (Display Advanced Editing Toolbar): **Tools** > **Advanced Editing** > **Advanced Editing Toolbar**

Menu (Display Advanced Editing Toolbar): **Alt+T-A-B** (Figure 6.13). The Advanced Editing Toolbar looks slightly different in Version 7.0 (it has an additional "3D" tool). See Figure 6.14.

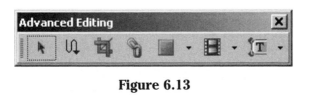

Figure 6.13

Figure 6.14

§ 6.2.2 Creating Links—Version 6.0

Links can be created directly from text and images using the Select Text tool or the Select Image tool. Using the Select Text tool insures that links are matched to exact text and provides uniform link sizing. Links can also be created on any space in a PDF file; that means that you can build links within image-only documents. To create a link using the Link tool:

1. Go to the location in the document where you want the link.
2. Select the **Link** tool on the Advanced Editing toolbar (the pointer becomes a cross hair [+], and any existing links in the document, including invisible links, are temporarily visible).
3. Drag the mouse to create a rectangle (this is the area in which the link is active).
4. The **Create Link** dialog box appears (Figure 6.15). Do *one* of the following:
   a. Select **Open a page in this document,** select the destination page number for the link, and set the page magnification
   b. Select **Open a file**, click **Browse** to select the destination file, and click **Select**
5. Click **OK.**

To create a link that connects to a Web page, perform the above steps, but rather than selecting **Open a file** or **Open a page in this document**:

Select **Open a web page,** and provide the URL of the destination Web page.

To create a link using the Select Text tool or the Select Image tool:

1. Select the **Select Text** tool or the **Select Image** tool.
2. Drag to select the text or image from which you want to create a link.
3. Right-click and choose **Create Link**, then do *one* of the following:
   a. Select **Open a page in this document,** and select the destination page number for the link

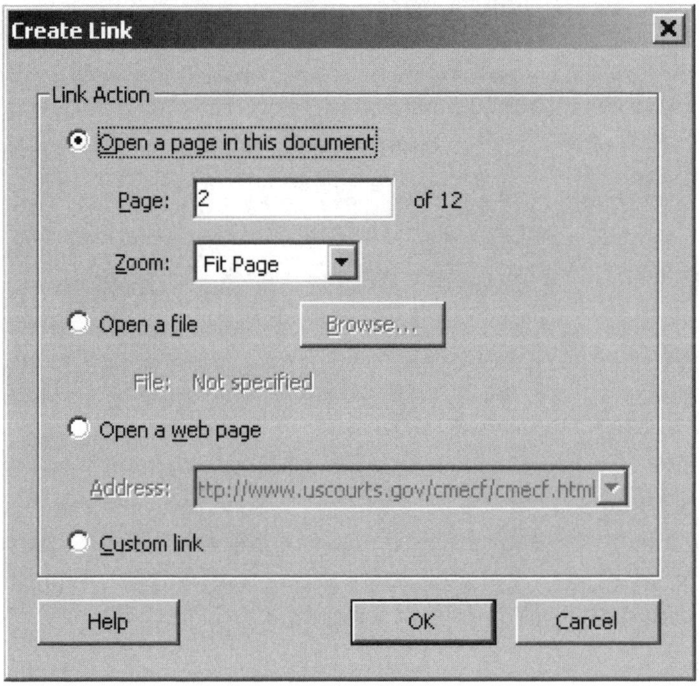

Figure 6.15

> b. Select **Open a file**, click **Browse** to select the destination file, and click **Select**
>
> c. Select **Open a web page**, and provide the URL of the destination Web page (Figure 6.16)
>
> 4. Click **OK** to set the link.

§ 6.2.3 Creating Links—Version 7.0

Creating links in Version 7.0 differs little from the process described above. However, the dialog boxes are just different enough to warrant an independent section describing the link creation process in Version 7.0.

Links can be created directly from text and images using the Select Text tool or the Select Image tool. Using the **Select Text** tool insures that Links are matched to exact text and provides uniform link sizing. Links can also be created on any space in a PDF document; that means that you can build Links within image-only documents. To create a link using the **Link** tool:

◆ Go to the location in the document where you want the Link

◆ Select the **Link** tool on the **Advanced Editing** toolbar (the pointer becomes a cross hair [+], and any existing links in the document, including invisible links, are temporarily visible)

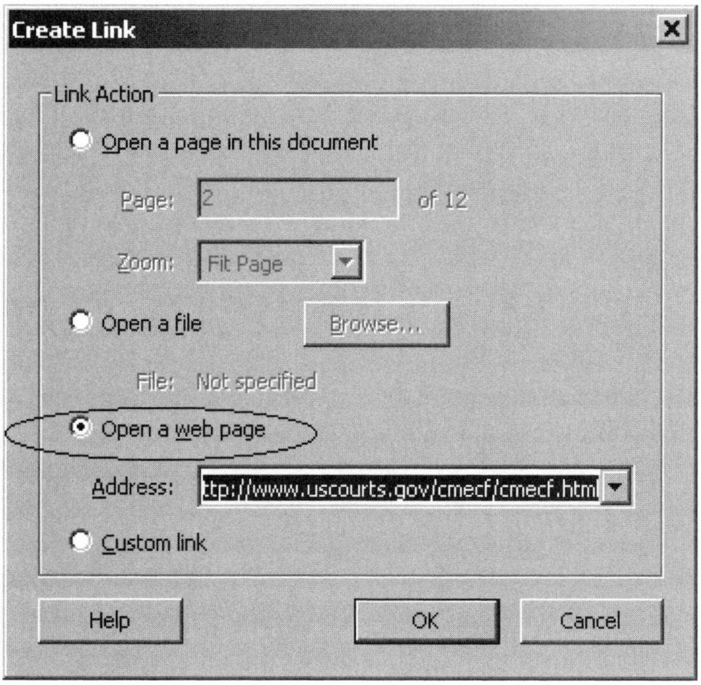

Figure 6.16

- ◆ Drag the mouse to create a rectangle (this is the area in which the link is active)
- ◆ The **Create Link** dialog box will appear. Do one of the following:
  - ◆ In the **Link Appearance** section select a **Link Appearance** from the drop down menu (Visible Rectangle or Invisible Rectangle)
  - ◆ **TIP**: Invisible rectangle links are unobtrusive in that there is no "box" around the link, but the reader of the document will not know that a link exists at a given location without some other indication, such as a change in font color.
  - ◆ In the **Link Action** section select the desired action (**Go To a Page View, Open a File, Open a Web Page,** or **Custom Link**); what you see when you click **Next** will depend on the type of action selected.
  - ◆ If you selected **Go To a Page View,** the **Create Go to View** dialog box appears and instructs you to "Use the scrollbars, mouse and zoom tools to select the target view, then press **Set Link** to create the link destination." Okay, this calls for a couple of TIPS.

    TIP 1: If you know you will be creating numerous links within a document (not linking to external documents), you can speed the link creation process by bookmarking the Link destination pages before you start creating the Links. With bookmarks in place, when the

Create Go to View dialog box appears all you have to do is click on the Bookmark for the desired destination and *presto!* you are there and ready to click the **Set Link** button (this eliminates lots of scrolling, page clicking, or guessing at page numbers).

TIP 2: In addition to using the scroll bars and mouse you can: Use the next-page and previous-page buttons to navigate to the desired page; Use the **Go To Page** command (**Ctrl+Shift+N** then specify page number).

◆ If you chose **Open a File**, clicking **Next** brings up a file open dialog box that allows you to browse for the file to be opened by the link.

To create a link that connects to a Web page, perform the above steps, but rather than selecting **Go To a Page View** or **Open a File**:

◆ Select **Open a Web Page**, click **Next** and provide the URL of the destination Web page.

To create a link using the **Select Text** tool or the **Select Image** tool:

◆ Select the **Select Text** tool or the **Select Image** tool
◆ Drag to select the text or image from which you want to create a link
◆ Right-click and choose **Create Link,** the **Create Link** dialog box will appear (Figure 6.16). From this point the procedure is the same as creating a link using the **Link Tool** described above.

§ 6.2.4 Setting the Appearance of Links

You can set the link appearance before or after you create the link—you choose. You can set the appearance of links using the Properties bar or by right-clicking on the link, then selecting the **Appearance** tab in the **Properties** dialog box. To display the Link Properties bar, select a link, then:

Menu (Display Links Properties Bar): **View** > **Toolbars** > **Properties Bar**

Keystroke (Display Links Property Bar): **Ctrl+E**

You can reuse the appearance settings of a link for all subsequent links in the document by right-clicking the link and selecting **Use Current Appearance as New Default.**

The Properties dialog box must be used to define the visibility of a link; the visibility of a link cannot be set in the Properties toolbar.

You can specify whether a link is visible or invisible, and lock the settings to prevent accidental changes.

◆ Select **Invisible Rectangle for Link Type** if you do not want users to see the link in the PDF document (invisible links are useful over photographs or graphics), or if you color code the text of the link.

◆ Select the **Locked** option in the **Appearance** tab of the **Properties** dialog box to prevent users from accidentally changing settings.

§ 6.2.5 Link Properties

Link properties are reused when you create new links, until you change the properties again. You can edit a link at any time. You can change its appearance, hotspot area, or associated link action; delete or resize the link rectangle; or change the destination of the link. Changing the properties of an existing link affects only the currently selected link. You can change the properties of several links at once if you select the links using the Link tool or the Select Object tool.

§ 6.2.6 Moving and Resizing Links

To move a link rectangle:

1. Select the **Link** tool or the **Select Object** tool.
2. Move the pointer over the link rectangle (the cross hair [+] changes to an arrow when the cursor is over a corner).
3. Drag the link to the desired new location.

To resize a link:

1. Select the **Link** tool or the **Select Object** tool.
2. Move the pointer over the link rectangle (the cross hair [+] changes to an arrow when the cursor is over a corner).
3. Drag any corner point until the rectangle is the desired size.

§ 6.2.7 Deleting Links

Any link in a PDF document can be deleted, or all links can be deleted at once. To delete a single link:

Select the **Link** tool or the **Select Object** tool, click on the link rectangle to be deleted, and then Press the **Delete** key.

To delete all links in a document:

Select the **Link** tool or the **Select Object** tool
Right-click on any link

Select **Edit > Select All** (all links in the document will be selected)
Press the **Delete** key (all links in the document will be deleted)

§ 6.2.8 Link Destinations

A destination is the end point of a link represented by text in the Destinations tab (where the user goes when the link is clicked). Destinations allow you to set navigation paths across a collection of PDF documents. Linking to a destination is recommended when linking across documents because, unlike a link to a page, a link to a destination is not affected by the addition or deletion of pages within the target document. The destinations of all links within a document can be displayed using the Links Destination list. To display the Link Destinations list:

Menu (View Link Destinations List): **View** > **Navigation Tabs** > **Destinations**

Keystroke (View Link Destinations List): **Alt+V-N-D**

When the Link Destination list appears, in Version 6.0, do *one* of the following:

a) Choose **Scan Document** from the **Options** menu
b) Click the **Scan Document** button at the top of the **Destinations** tab.

In Version 7.0, opening the Link Destinations dialog box automatically scans the document for existing links.

To sort the destinations, in the Link Destination list, do *one* of the following:

a) To sort destination names alphabetically, pull down the **Options** list and select **Sort by Name**
b) To sort destinations by page number, pull down the **Options** list and select **Sort by Page**

To change or delete a destination using the Links Destination list, select a destination, right-click, and do *one* of the following:

a) To move to the target location, choose **Go to Destination**
b) To delete the destination, choose **Delete**
c) To reset the target of the destination to the page displayed, choose **Set Destination**
d) To give the destination a different name, choose **Rename**

To create and link a destination in the same or another PDF document using the Links Destination list:

1. In the target document, click **Scan Document** under **Options** in the Links Destination list.
2. Navigate to the location where you want to create a destination. (Note: In Version 6.0 you must scan a document for any existing destinations before you can create a new destination. This step is required, even when you are creating the first destination for the document. In Version 7.0, opening the Link Destinations dialog box automatically scans the document for existing links.)

3. Set the destination by doing *one* of the following:
   a. Choose **New Destination** from the **Options** menu
   b. Click the **Create New Destination** button at the top of the **Destinations** tab
4. Type the name of the destination, and press **Enter** (Note: a destination name must be unique).
5. In the source document (the document you want to create the link from), select the **Link** tool.
6. Drag a rectangle to specify a source for the link.
7. In the **Create Link** dialog box, select **Custom Link** and click **OK.**
8. On the **Actions** tab of the **Link Properties** dialog box, select **Go to a page in this document** (if you're linking to a destination in the same document) or **Go to a page in another document** (if you're linking to a destination in another document) from the **Select Action** menu, and click **Add.**
9. If you are linking to another document, in the **Go to a page in another document** dialog box, select your target file (the file in which you defined the destination). In the **Open in** menu, specify how the target document should open.
10. Select **Use Named Destination,** and browse to select your named destination. Click **OK,** and click **OK** again.

§ 6.2.9 Link Security

Now that you know how easy it is to change link properties (name, destination, and so on), maybe you don't want other users to change your links. Basic PDF file security can be used to restrict the ability of others to make changes (See Figures 6.10, 6.11 and 6.17).

In the **Password Security—Settings** dialog box, setting **Changes Allowed** (in the **Permissions** section) to **None** requires other users to enter the correct password before link properties can be changed.

§ 6.3 Page Numbering

You may notice that the page numbers on the document pages do not always match the page numbers that appear below the page thumbnails and in the status bar. Pages are numbered with integers, starting with page 1 for the first page of the document, and so on. Because some PDF documents may contain front matter, such as a copyright page and table of contents, their body pages may not follow the numbering shown in the status bar. Or, as may happen in the legal setting, you may want a PDF document to have page numbers that correspond to Bates numbers or record index numbers.

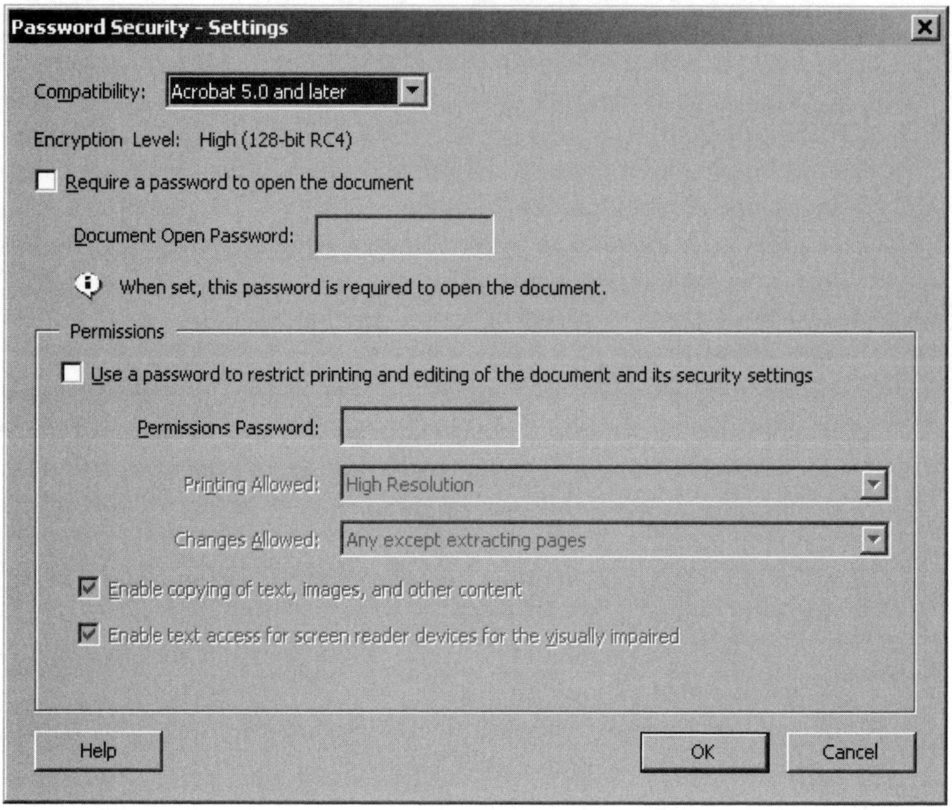

Figure 6.17

Acrobat uses two types of page numbers: printed page numbering (actual; in the top-half of the Page Numbering dialog box), and online page numbering (virtual; in the bottom-half of the Page Numbering dialog box). By setting the online page numbers to correspond with record index pages or Bates numbers, Go To (Ctrl+Shift+N) can be used to navigate PDF files according to those number systems. An example illustrating the use of online page number might be useful. Consider a matter where you have an appellate record (or appendix) that consists of five volumes. Each volume contains approximately five hundred pages. Thus, the pages in Volume III will be in the approximate range of 1,500 through 2,000. In order to be able to Go To page 1,665 in Volume III, the online page numbers in that document need to be reset to begin at 1,500—likewise for discovery documents. Assume five notebooks of documents, each containing approximately five hundred pages. Each notebook was scanned as a separate PDF file. Each page in all five files has been sequentially Bates numbered. In order to Go To page Bates number 1,776 in the file covering that page range, the online page numbers must be set to commence with the first Bates number in that document.

To set online page numbers to correspond to volume page numbers:

1. In the **Pages** tab of the navigation pane (Figure 6.18), choose **Number Pages** from the **Options** menu
2. In the **Pages** section (top half of **Page Numbering** dialog box; see Figure 6.19), select **All.**
3. In the **Numbering** section (bottom half of the **Page Numbering** dialog box; see Figure 6.20), do the following:
   i. Select **Begin new section.**
   ii. Choose a **Style** (1, 2, 3 works well).
   iii. Type in a **Prefix,** if desired.
   iv. Type the **Start** number (for example, **1552**).
   v. Click **OK.**

To test the new online page number system, use the Go To function (**Ctrl+Shift+N**), type in an appropriate online page number, and press **Enter**; the destination should correspond to the appropriate Bates number or record index page number.

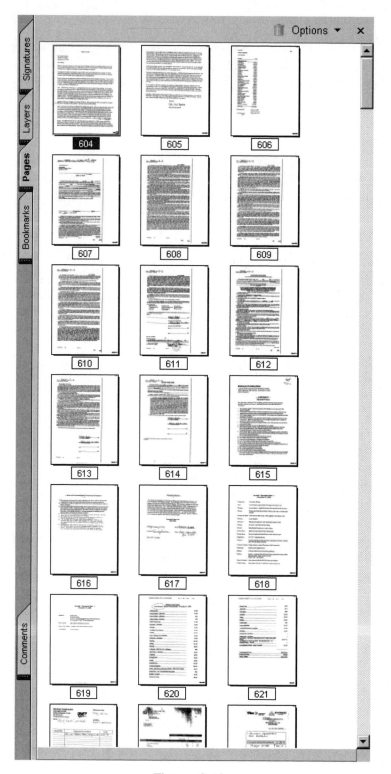

Figure 6.18

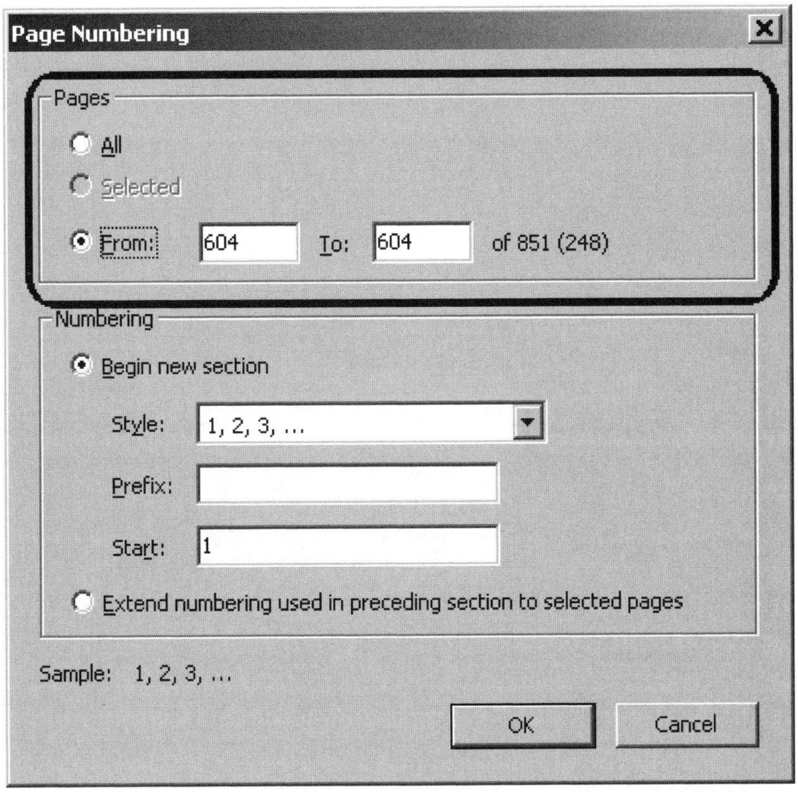

Figure 6.19

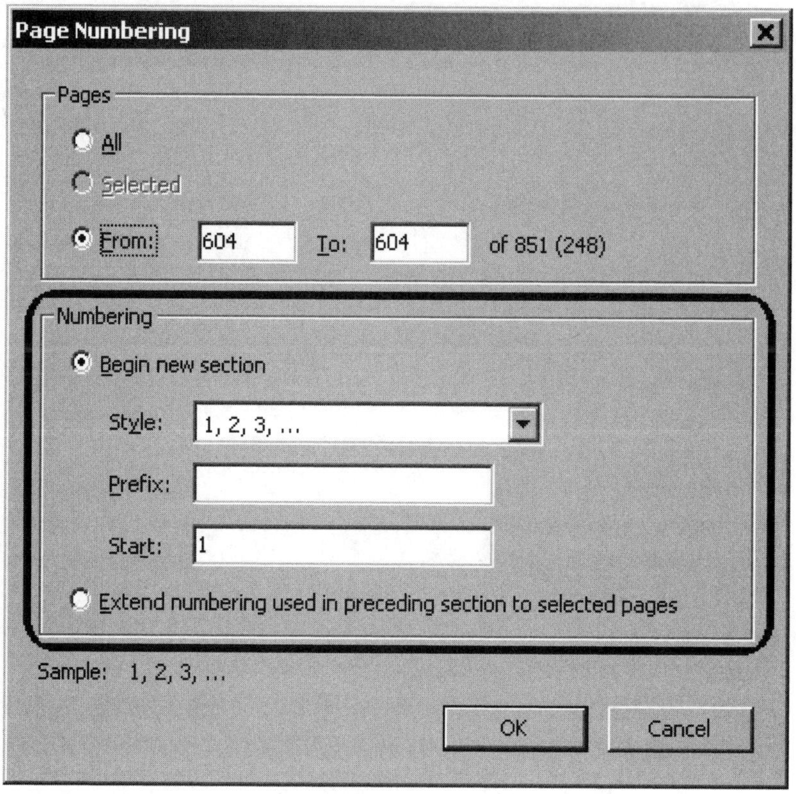

Figure 6.20

Commenting Tools

7

Information, information, information; lawyers process information (remember Chapter 1?). Historically, much of the information processed by lawyers existed in paper form. One of the barriers to working with information that has been converted from paper to digital form is the loss of familiar tools like highlighters and sticky notes. Acrobat removes this barrier with a full palette of commenting tools.

In Acrobat, a "comment" refers to a note, highlighting, or any other markup added to a PDF file using one or more of the commenting tools. Notes are probably the most useful and commonly used comment. Think of notes as electronic Post-it® Notes. The Note tool lets you add the equivalent of a sticky note to your PDF file just as you would with a paper document. Text box comments are a great way to annotate drawings and diagrams. You can also add stamps and draw shapes. Comments can be placed anywhere in the PDF file, and you determine the style and format of the comments. The tools to create comments are located on the Commenting and Advanced Commenting toolbars. If your comments are too long to fit in a note or text box, you can put lengthy remarks into an attached file. If you need to comment with something more powerful than mere words, sound and video clips can be attached as well.

Because notes and text boxes are comments, their content can be searched for in Acrobat or across a range of files using Windows Explorer. Additionally, because notes and text boxes are comments, they appear in the comment pane at the bottom of the work area with a simple click on the Comments tab. If you want to review the comments that have been added to a thousand pages of discovery documents, simply open the PDF file in Acrobat and click on the **Comments** tab, and a list of all comments appears (Figure 7.1).

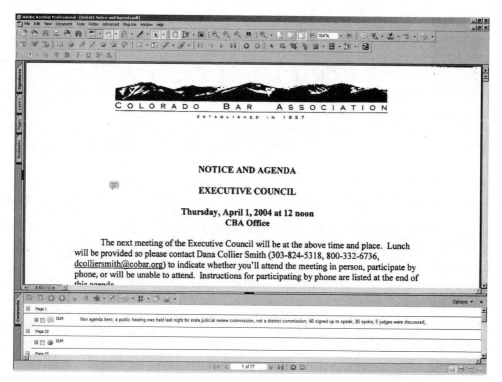

Figure 7.1

If you want to see only note comments, click on the **Filter comments displayed** button at the top of the comments window and select **Show by Type > Notes** (Figure 7.2). The comment filter looks a bit different in Version 7.0, but works essentially the same way. See Figure 7.3.

If you see a comment in the comments window and want to go the page in the document, simply double-click the comment and the location of the comment is displayed.

§ 7.1 Commenting Toolbars

To add comments to a PDF file, you begin with either the Commenting toolbar (Figure 7.4) or the Advanced Commenting toolbar (Figure 7.5).

To display the Commenting toolbar:

> Menu (Display Commenting Toolbar): **Tools** > **Commenting** > **Show Commenting Toolbar**
> or

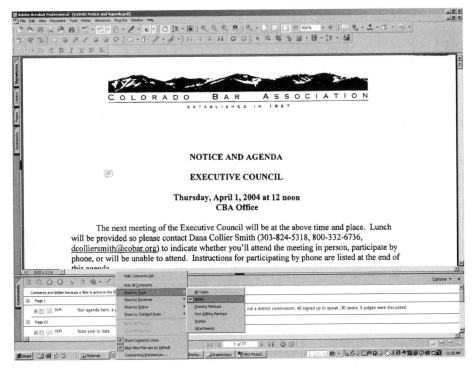

Figure 7.2

Figure 7.3

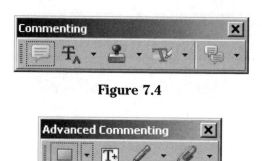

Figure 7.4

Figure 7.5

View > **Toolbars** > **Commenting**
Keystroke (Display Commenting Toolbar): **Alt+T-C-B** or **Alt+V-T-C**

To display the Advanced Commenting toolbar:

Menu (Display Advanced Commenting Toolbar): **Tools** > **Advanced Commenting** > **Show Advanced Commenting Toolbar**
or
View > **Toolbars** > **Advanced Commenting**
Keystroke (Display Advanced Commenting Toolbar): **Alt+T-V-B** or **Alt+V-T-V**

To select a commenting tool, click the tool on the Commenting or Advanced Commenting toolbar, or click the arrow next to a tool, and then select a tool from the menu.

§ 7.2 Notes

Notes are the most commonly used comment. You can use the Note tool to add notes on any page in a PDF file, you can position them anywhere on the page, and you can add as many to notes to each page as you want. When you add a note, an icon and a pop-up window appear. You can add bold, italics, and other attributes to the text in the pop-up window, similar to formatting text in a word processing application. If you enter more text than fits in the pop-up window, the text wraps. You can also resize the window, if desired.

To add a note comment:

1. Select the **Note** tool in the **Commenting** toolbar. (See Figure 7.6).
2. Click the location where you want to place the note.
3. Type the text for the note in the pop-up window (You can use the **Select Text** tool to copy and paste text from an image-on-text PDF document into the note).

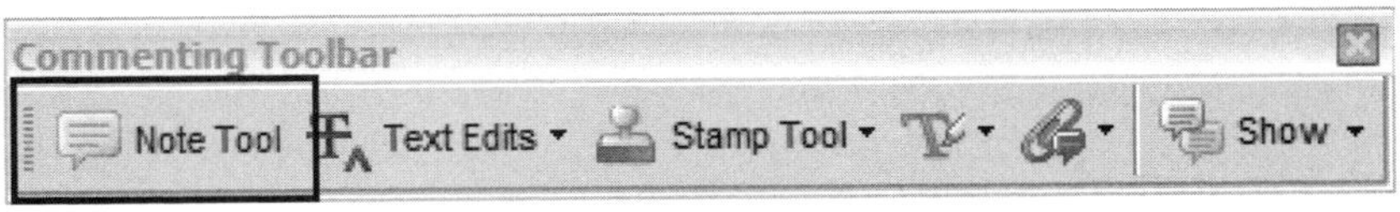

Figure 7.6

4. If desired, click the **Close** box in the upper right corner of the pop-up window to close the note (closing the pop-up window does not delete the note).

If you don't want the Note tool to switch to the Hand tool after you add a note, select the **Keep Tool Selected** option in the Properties toolbar. To display the Properties toolbar, right-click the toolbar area, and then choose **Properties Bar.** When you select the Note tool, the **Keep Tool Selected** option appears.

To edit a note:

1. Click or double-click the **Note** icon to open the pop-up window.
2. Edit the text as needed. When finished, click the **Close** box in the upper right corner of the pop-up window, or click anywhere outside the pop-up window.
3. Use the Properties toolbar to change the text formatting, note color, and other note properties.

To resize a pop-up window, drag the lower right corner of the window to the appropriate size. Use the Commenting panel in the Preferences dialog box to change the font size, default pop-up behavior, and other settings for creating and viewing comments.

To delete a note:

Select the **Note** tool or the **Hand** tool, and do *one* of the following:

a) Click on the **Note** icon, then press **Delete**
b) Right-click the **Note** icon or the title bar of the pop-up window, and select **Delete**
c) Right-click the text area of the pop-up window, and select **Delete Comment**

The properties that you set for a Note can be selected as the default properties for all future Notes. So, if you want your Notes to be yellow, your paralegal's Notes to be green, and your associate's Notes to be blue, this can be quickly and easily accomplished. In Version 6.0, right-click on the Note and select "Make Current Properties Default." In Version 7.0, you must first close the pop-up (click the "x" in the upper-right corner of the Note) then right click the remaining Note icon and select "Make Current Properties Default." See Figure 7.7.

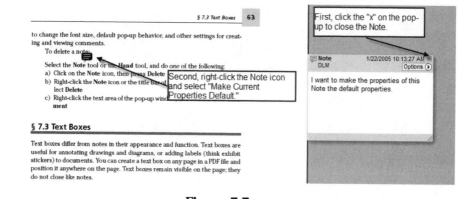

Figure 7.7

§ 7.3 Text Boxes

Text boxes differ from notes in their appearance and function. Text boxes are useful for annotating drawings and diagrams, or adding labels (think exhibit stickers) to documents. You can create a text box on any page in a PDF file and position it anywhere on the page. Text boxes remain visible on the page; they do not close like notes.

Text boxes are created using (you guessed it) the Text Box tool. When you click a text box to select it, you can use the options on the Properties toolbar to format the fill and border of the text box. When you double-click a text box, you can use the options on the Properties toolbar to format the text inside the Text box. An example of a text box exhibit label appears in Figure 7.8.

Figure 7.8

To add a Text Box, display the Advanced Commenting toolbar, then:

1. Select the **Text Box** tool.
2. Click the location for the text box (alternatively, drag a rectangle to define the boundaries of the text box).
3. Use the Properties toolbar to change the color, alignment, and font attributes of the text, and then type the text (to display the Properties toolbar, right-click the toolbar area and select **Properties**).

As with Notes, the properties that you set for a Text Box can be selected as the default properties for all future Text Boxes. So, if you want your Text

Boxes to be yellow with black text, the Text Boxes added by your paralegal to be dark green with white text, and the Text Boxes of your associate to be light blue with black text, this can be quickly and easily accomplished. After setting the desired properties, right-click on the Text Box and select "Make Current Properties Default."

To resize a text box, select the box using the Hand tool or the Text Box tool, and then drag one of the corners to the desired size.

§ 7.4 Callout Text Boxes

Callout text boxes are great for annotating documents for use as exhibits, or for creating charts and drawings. Callout text boxes are really just text boxes that you connect to an area of the document with an arrow. To create a call-out text box in Version 6.0:

Callout Text Boxes can be placed anywhere on the page. Both the "box" and the "pointer" can be moved and the connecting lines automatically adjust.

1. Select the **Text Box** tool, and then draw a box near the area the annotation applies to.
2. Type the text in the text box.
3. Select the **Arrow** tool from the drawing tools menu on the Advanced Commenting toolbar.
4. Draw *from* the area where you want the arrow, *to* a point on the side of the text box by left-clicking and dragging the pointer to the desired position.
5. Using the **Hand** tool, select the arrow markup, then select options from the Properties toolbar or the Properties dialog box to change the appearance of the arrow (hint: select the same color and appearance for the text box and Arrow tool).

Callout boxes are so handy that Adobe added at Callout Tool in Version 7.0. To create a Callout Text Box in Version 7.0, simply click on the **Callout Tool** (located on the Drawing Markups Toolbar; see Figure 7.9), move your pointer to the approximate location on the page where you want the arrow to be and click. A **Callout Text Box** will be created. You can now insert text in the box, drag the box to a new location, and drag the pointer end of the arrow to a new location (the connecting lines will automatically adjust). See Figure 7.10.

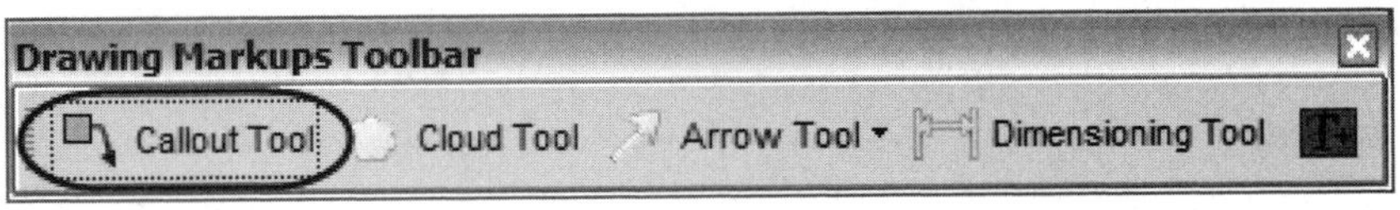

Figure 7.9

§ 7.4 Callout Text Boxes

Callout text boxes are great for annotating documents for use as exhibits, or for creating charts and drawings. Callout text boxes are really just text boxes that you connect to an area of the document with an arrow. To create a callout text box:

1. Select the **Text Box** tool, and then draw [ ] annotation applies to.
2. Type the text in the text box.
3. Select the **Arrow** tool from the drawing [ ]anced
   Commenting toolbar.
4. Draw *from* the area where you want the arrow, to a point on the side
   of the text box by left-clicking and dragging the pointer to the desired
   position.
5. Using the **Hand** tool, select the arrow markup, then select options
   from the Properties toolbar or the Properties dialog box to change the
   appearance of the arrow (hint: select the same color and appearance
   for the text box and Arrow tool).

> Callout Text Boxes can be placed anywhere on the page. Both the "box" and the "pointer" can be moved and the connecting lines automatically adjust.

Figure 7.10

§ 7.5 Text Markup

The Highlighter tool, Cross-Out Text tool, and the Underline Text tool do what their names suggest. The functions of the text markup tools come within Adobe's definition of comments, so their use and attributes are much like notes and text boxes. However, unlike notes and text boxes, these markup tools work only with image-on-text PDF files. This type of comment may be used independently or in conjunction with notes. For example, you may want to highlight a section of text, and then double-click the highlighting to add a note window.

To highlight, cross out, or underline text:

1. On the Commenting toolbar, select a tool (**Highlighter, Cross-Out Text**, or **Underline Text**).
2. Move the cursor to the beginning of the text to be marked up, then click and drag (use **Ctrl+drag** to mark a rectangular area of text; this is especially useful to mark up text in a column).

To associate a note with the highlighted or underlined text, select the **Hand** tool and double-click the markup. Type the text in the pop-up window that appears.

To delete a highlight, cross out, or underline markup, do *one* of the following:

a) Right-click the markup and select **Delete**

b) Select the **Hand** tool, click the markup, then press **Delete**

§ 7.6 Dimensioning Tool

Acrobat 7.0 adds another new feature with the **Dimensioning Tool** (located on the Drawing Markups Toolbar; see Figure 7.11). If you use the line, box, or other shape drawing tools to create diagrams, then you may find the Dimensioning Tool helpful. Simply click on the tool, click and drag the pointer between the points that you want to show dimensions for. When you stop dragging and release the button on your pointing device, the text insertion point will be in the middle of the new dimension line ready for you to insert the appropriate text (typically a number stating the distance that the line represents).

Figure 7.11

§ 7.7 Comment Summaries

The ability to summarize comments using Acrobat is a powerful tool for lawyers. Think of a thousand or ten thousand pages of discovery documents. No, they are not in notebooks or boxes; these pages have been scanned and exist as one or more PDF files. Start turning the pages and adding notes or text boxes as you go. Now, after reviewing those thousand or ten thousand pages and adding a hundred or a thousand sticky notes, all of the text in every note or text box can be extracted in a matter of seconds to a new PDF document.

When you summarize comments, you can either create a new PDF file with comments that can be printed, or you can print the summary directly. The summary is not associated with or linked to the PDF file that the comments come from. If **Print Comment Pop-ups** is selected in the Commenting panel of the Preferences dialog box (see Section 7.10), note pop-ups appear on the printed pages when you select **File** > **Print.** The Print with Comments command provides more control over how the comments are printed than the Print command.

To create a comment summary:

6.0 Menu (Summarize Comments): **Document** > **Summarize Comments**
6.0 Keystroke (Summarize Comments): **Alt+D-S**

7.0 Menu (Summarize Comments): **Comments** > **Summarize Comments**

7.0 Keystroke (Summarize Comments): **Alt+C-Z**

To print a comment summary:

Keystroke (Print Comments): **File** > **Print with Comments**

Whether creating or printing a comment summary, the Summarize Options dialog box appears. In this box you can

♦ Specify how to lay out the comments on the page
♦ Choose how to sort the comments
♦ Select whether you want all comments to appear in the summary, or only the comments that are currently showing

If you created a summary, a separate PDF document appears. You can save or print this document. If you want to summarize the comments again, switch back to the original document using the Windows menu or typing **Ctrl+F6.** Comments can be printed or summarized directly without opening the Summarize Options dialog box by selecting **Print Comments Summary** or **Create PDF of Comments Summary** from the Print Comments menu in the Comments list. Choose **More Options** from this menu to specify the summary settings to be used.

Comment summaries work best for notes, text boxes, and marked-up text because these summaries contain text. Because the drawing markup tools (graphic shapes) are also comments, those markups are also included in the comment summary. If you use the drawing tools to mark up image-only files, the comment summary provides a list of where you drew lines and shapes (which is really not very useful).

§ 7.8 Lines and Shapes

The drawing tools are used to mark up PDF files with lines, circles, and other shapes; these are called drawing markups. Why would you want to draw on your documents? (You're a lawyer, after all.) Well, recall the different types of PDF files: image-only and image-on-text. When working with image-only files (think discovery documents that have been scanned to PDF) there is no text to select for marking up. With the drawing tools you can draw lines around portions of an image; in other words, you can draw lines (round, rectangular, polygonal) over, under, beside, and around the picture of the text. While there may be no text to highlight, you can draw a line over, under, or around what looks like text (or any other portion of the image). The drawing tools are really powerful when working with image-only files. You can make them even more powerful by adding text or a note to any drawing markup.

Acrobat includes a number of drawing markup tools. At the risk of stating the obvious, here is what they are and what they do:

- Rectangle tool—draws rectangles (hold down Shift while using this tool to draw squares)
- Oval tool—draws ovals (hold down Shift while using this tool to draw circles)
- Arrow tool—draws straight lines with arrows on either or both ends
- Line tool—draws straight lines
- Polygon tool—creates a closed shape with multiple segments (great for sketching odd shaped objects)
- Polygonal Line tool—creates an open shape (line) with multiple segments
- Cloud tool—same as the Polygon tool, but the segments turn into a cloud shape when you finish drawing
- Dimensioning Tool—Acrobat 7.0 adds another new feature with the Dimensioning Tool (located on the Drawing Markups Toolbar; see Figure 7.11). If you use the line, box, or other shape drawing tools to create diagrams, then you may find the Dimensioning Tool helpful.

To use the drawing tools in Version 6.0, display the Advanced Commenting toolbar (in Version 7.0, the drawing tools are on the Drawing Markups Toolbar; see Figure 7.11, above), then select a drawing tool from the drawing menu:

- To draw a rectangle or oval, left-click and drag across the area where you want the drawing shape to appear
- To draw a line, left-click and drag across the area where you want the line to appear
- To draw an arrow, left-click and drag across the area where you want the line with an arrow to appear (note: the arrow pointer appears where you begin drawing)
- To draw a polygon or polygon line, left-click a starting point (note: left-click only, not left-click and drag), move the mouse pointer and click to create a segment of the polygon, then continue moving the mouse pointer and clicking to create additional segments of the polygon
  - When finished drawing a polygon, click the starting point or double-click to close the shape
  - Double-click to end a polygon line
- To draw a cloud, left-click a starting point (note: left-click only, not left-click and drag), move the mouse pointer and click to create a segment of the cloud shape, then continue moving the mouse pointer and clicking to create additional segments of the cloud
- When finished drawing a closed shape, click the starting point or double-click to close the shape

◆ To draw a dimension line, click on the dimension tool, click and drag the pointer between the points that you want to show dimensions for. When you stop dragging and release the button on your pointing device, the text insertion point will be in the middle of the new dimension line ready for you to insert the appropriate text (typically a number stating the distance that the line represents).

To hold the tool steady when drawing a straight or diagonal line, press Shift while drawing the markup. Release Shift only after releasing the mouse button.

To delete a drawing markup:

◆ Right-click the drawing markup, and select **Delete**

To change the appearance of a drawing markup:

◆ Right-click the drawing markup, select **Properties,** then change options on the **Appearances** tab

Tip: Use the drawing tools to create charts and diagrams on a blank page. To create a blank-page PDF document, use a word processing application and print a blank page with the desired margin settings to PDF.

Tip: After the first use of a drawing tool, right-click the drawing to set the Properties as desired. Then right-click again, this time selecting **Make Current Properties Default.**

Tip: Setting the opacity of the drawing markup tools to 50 percent allows them to be used as a highlighter on image-only PDF files. This can be a hugely powerful tool for lawyer work with image-only PDF files.

§ 7.9 Stamps

Stamps can be handy for marking PDF documents as draft, confidential, received, and so on. Acrobat comes with a set of ready-made stamps, both static and dynamic. An example of a static stamp is one that applies "RECEIVED" to a document. The dynamic RECEIVED stamp includes the user's name (derived from the Identity section of the Preferences dialog box) along with the date and time when the stamp is applied. Acrobat allows you to create custom stamps that can contain text or images. A custom stamp that applies a facsimile of your signature can be especially useful (see Section 8.3). Bates numbering or Bates stamping is not done with an Acrobat stamp, but rather requires a plug-in (this is discussed in Chapter 13).

§ 7.9.1 Ready-Made Stamps

To use the ready-made stamps that come with Acrobat, first select the desired stamp. To select a specific stamp, click on the drop-down arrow on the right next to the Stamp tool, navigate to the desired category (Dynamic, **Personal,** Sign Here or Standard Business), then highlight the desired stamp. The pointer takes on the shape of a conventional rubber stamp; place the pointer where you want to apply the stamp and left-click. To use the same stamp again, click on the Stamp tool on the Commenting toolbar (Figure 7.12), point, and click.

Figure 7.12

Figure 7.13 below illustrates custom-made stamps.

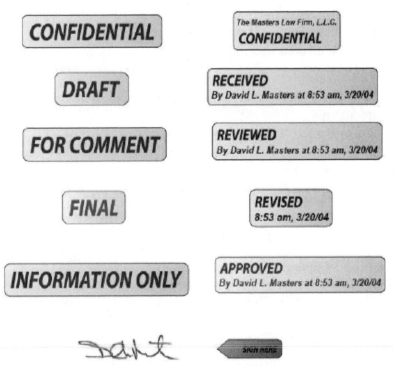

Figure 7.13

§ 7.9.2 Custom-Made Stamps

You can create custom stamps for a variety of purposes; think of all the rubber stamps in your office and you'll begin to see the possibilities. Custom stamps can be created from PDF files or from any common graphic format. When you select the file to be used for the stamp, you can add it to an existing category or you can create a new one.

To create a custom stamp follow the steps described below. While the steps described below may appear inconsistent with the menu choices in both Acrobat 6.0 and 7.0, they will provide guidance for creating custom stamps. If you pull down the **Tools** menu, select **Commenting**, then select **Stamps**, and then select **Create Custom Stamp**, you will be presented with a dialog box that does not offer the option to "create" a new stamp. The same result follows if you use the pull-down menu on the stamp tool button and select **Create Custom Stamp**. As you will see, and as described below, when you select **Manage Stamps** the dialog box has a button (option) to "create" a new custom stamp.

Before you begin the process of creating a custom stamp, you will need the artwork that will be applied by the stamp. The artwork should be an image file (JPEG, TIFF, etc.) or an existing PDF file. It goes without saying that you need to know where the artwork file resides on your computer or network, so if you create many stamps it may be helpful to create a folder where all stamp artwork will be located.

With these preliminaries out of the way, to create a custom stamp:

6.0 Menu (Create Custom Stamp): **Tools** > **Commenting** > **Stamp Tool** > **Manage Stamps**

6.0 Keystroke (Create Custom Stamp): **Alt+T-C-S-M**

7.0 Menu (Create Custom Stamp): **Tools** > **Commenting** > **Stamps** > **Manage Stamps**

7.0 Keystroke (Create Custom Stamp): **Alt+T-C-M-M**

Or, use the pull-down menu located next to the **Stamp Tool** on the commenting toolbar and select **Manage Stamps**. Then:

1. Click **Create.**
2. Click **Browse,** and double-click the file to be used as the stamp art (if the file has more than one page, select the page to use for the stamp).
3. Click **OK.**
4. For **Category,** select an existing category, or type a name to create a new category.
5. For **Name,** type the name that will appear on the Stamp menu on the Commenting toolbar.
6. Click **OK.**

Once applied to a PDF document, stamps can be resized, moved, or have their Properties modified.

§ 7.10 Deleting Comments

Comments (whether notes, text boxes, shapes, highlighting, and so on) can be deleted about as easily as they can be added. To delete a single comment, do *one* of the following:

- Right-click the comment and select **Delete**
- Select the **Hand** tool, click the comment, and press **Delete**

To delete multiple comments:

1. Click the **Comments** tab in the navigation pane (this displays the Comments list at the bottom of the screen).
2. Select the comments to be deleted (hold down the **Ctrl** key to click on and select multiple comments).
3. Click the **Trash** (delete) icon.

When deleting comments, note the following:

- If comments are placed on top of one another, deleting the comment may appear to do nothing, because the next item in the stack is still visible. You may need to delete several comments before they are all removed.
- If a comment is locked, you cannot delete it until you unlock it. To unlock a comment, right-click the comment, select **Properties,** deselect **Locked,** then click **Close.**

§ 7.11 Comment Properties

All of the comments described in this chapter (notes, text boxes, callout text boxes, text markups, lines, shapes, and stamps) have properties. Those properties can be modified for each individual comment by right-clicking, selecting **Properties**, and making adjustments. Many comment properties can be set universally to affect all comments by working with commenting preferences on the Edit menu. For example, comments can be made easier to read by selecting a larger font size, you can turn off connector lines or side-alignment, and you can set the Note tool to remain selected after a note has been added (if you don't want the Note tool to switch to the Hand tool after you add a note, select the **Keep Tool Selected** option in the Properties toolbar).

To set preferences for comments:

Menu (Edit Comment Preferences): **Edit** > **Preferences** (select **Commenting** in the left window)

Keystroke (Edit Comment Preferences): **Alt+E-N** (select **Commenting** in the left window) or **Ctrl+K**

Once the Edit Comment Preferences dialog box appears, there are a number of default settings that can be established. A brief description of each follows. In Version 7.0 the arrangement of the commenting default settings is a bit different, but the options are roughly the same.

§ 7.11.1 Font and Font Size

This determines the font and the size of text in pop-up windows. This setting applies to all new and existing comments.

§ 7.11.2 Pop-up Opacity

The value (between 0 and 100) determines the opacity of the comment pop-up windows. When the pop-up window is open but not selected, an opacity value of 100 makes the window opaque, while lower values make the window more transparent.

§ 7.11.3 Automatically Open Pop-ups on Mouse Rollover

When the mouse pointer is placed over a comment of any type, including drawing markups and stamps, the pop-up window opens.

§ 7.11.4 Print Comment Pop-ups

The pop-up windows associated with comments are printed. You may prefer using the Print with Comments command.

§ 7.11.5 Hide Comment Pop-ups when Comments List Is Open

Pop-up windows do not appear when the Comments list is displayed. This option helps reduce screen clutter when a page includes many comments.

§ 7.11.6 Show Indicator Arrows to Off-Screen Comments

Arrows indicate that off-screen comments are available.

§ 7.11.7 Show Comment Connecting Lines on Mouse Rollover

When the mouse pointer moves over a comment markup (such as highlighting or a note icon), the shaded connector line between the comment and the open pop-up window appears.

§ 7.11.8 Scale Document to Fit Pop-ups

Adjusts the page zoom so that pop-up windows outside the page boundaries fit within the current view.

§ 7.11.9 Scale Document to Fit Comments

Adjusts the page zoom so that comments outside the page boundaries fit within the current view. This option applies to all comments except pop-up windows.

§ 7.11.10 Open Pop-up when Comment Is Selected

A pop-up window appears when you click the note icon or comment markup.

§ 7.11.11 Automatically Open Pop-ups for Comments other than Notes

A pop-up window appears when you create a new comment using a drawing tool, the Text Box tool, or the Pencil tool. This can be useful for adding commentary when using the drawing tools to highlight portions of image-only files.

§ 7.11.12 Copy Encircled Text into Drawing Comment Pop-ups

The pop-up windows associated with drawing comments, such as those created by the Rectangle tool, include any text within the comment if this option is selected.

§ 7.11.13 Copy Selected Text into Highlight, Cross-out, and Underline Comment Pop-ups

The pop-up window associated with proofreading markup comments, such as those created by the Highlighter tool, include any text to which the comment is applied if this option is selected.

§ 7.12 Final Comment on Comments

The ease of use and power of comments in Acrobat will likely be the feature to convince you that working with digital documents beats dealing with paper hands down. The ability to search for text in comments, not to mention the ability to summarize them, brings the power of your computer to bear on what has been at best more paper to keep track of. Remember, the text you add to PDF files, whether image-only or image-on-text PDF files, is included in searches performed and indexes maintained by third-party applications such as Windows Explorer. If you previously prepared written summaries of documents, you then had two documents to keep track of—the original and the summary. With Acrobat, comments can be part of the document, and they can be searched or summarized. And a digital document won't fall behind your desk or blow away with a gust of wind.

Digital Signatures

8

When you move beyond using Acrobat to simply organize, review, and comment on documents, and start using it for the delivery or exchange of original work product, the time has come to sign your documents. Most court-approved e-filing systems accept pleadings that are signed with a typed statement as simple as "Signed by David L. Masters." Not very professional or secure. There are basically two ways to use digital signatures with Acrobat: (1) secure digital signatures using Acrobat self-sign security or third-party digital signature applications, or (2) use an Acrobat custom stamp consisting of an image of your signature. The signature image used for a custom stamp can be used (displayed) in Acrobat self-sign secure digital signatures.

A digital signature, like a conventional handwritten signature, identifies the person signing a document. Unlike traditional signatures on paper, however, a true digital signature (as opposed to simple signature stamps) stores information "behind the scenes" about the person signing a document.

As a lawyer you may have concerns about the security of digital signatures. True digital signatures can be more secure than traditional handwritten signatures. After all, anyone can pick up a pen and sign your name to a document. Worse still, anyone can pick up your rubber stamp and apply your signature to a document. In other words, if someone wants to put your signature on a document, paper or electronic, they can probably do it. If you are among the truly paranoid, then you will want to use a secure third-party digital signature application or plug-in.

§ 8.1 Using Acrobat Digital Signatures

An Acrobat digital signature can appear as a logo or other image, or as text explaining the purpose of the signing. A digital signature can be either visible or invisible (Figure 8.1).

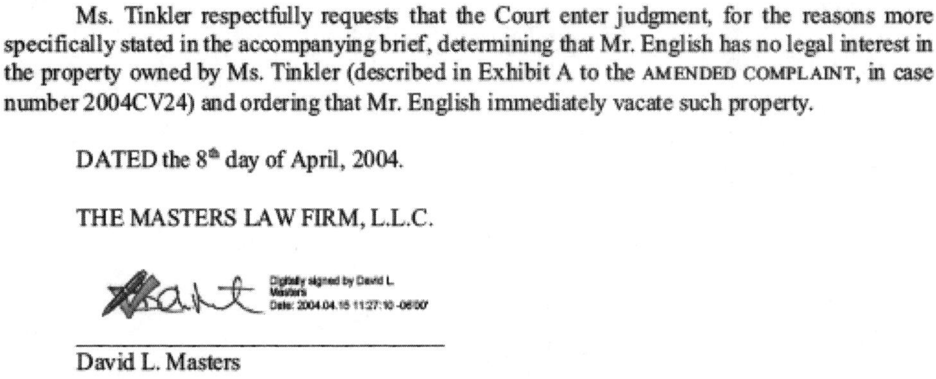

> Ms. Tinkler respectfully requests that the Court enter judgment, for the reasons more specifically stated in the accompanying brief, determining that Mr. English has no legal interest in the property owned by Ms. Tinkler (described in Exhibit A to the AMENDED COMPLAINT, in case number 2004CV24) and ordering that Mr. English immediately vacate such property.
>
> DATED the 8th day of April, 2004.
>
> THE MASTERS LAW FIRM, L.L.C.
>
> Digitally signed by David L. Masters
> Date: 2004.04.15 11:27:10 -06'00'
>
> _____
> David L. Masters

Figure 8.1

A visible signature appears in both the document and the Signatures tab. An invisible signature appears only in the Signatures tab (Figure 8.2).

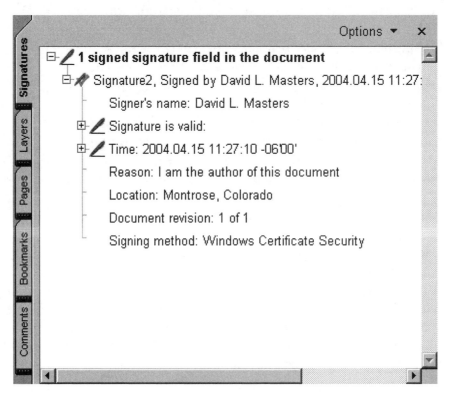

Figure 8.2

Before you can sign a document using an Acrobat digital signature, you must create or select a digital ID, which contains the signature information that you can share with other users in a certificate. A certificate is a confirmation of your digital ID and contains information used to protect data. You can create more than one digital ID if you sign documents in different roles or with different certification methods. When a digital signature is applied, a unique fingerprint with encrypted numbers is embedded in the document. The recipient needs the signer's certificate to validate that the digital signature and certificate match the signer's digital ID. Certificates can be sent via electronic mail to recipients who require the ability to validate signatures.

Secure digital signatures have one major drawback that might persuade you to use a less secure method such as a simple signature stamp. If you sign and send many documents to people who don't have your certificate, the signature will probably appear on their computer screen or the printed page with a question mark or message indicating that the signature has not been verified or validated (Figure 8.3).

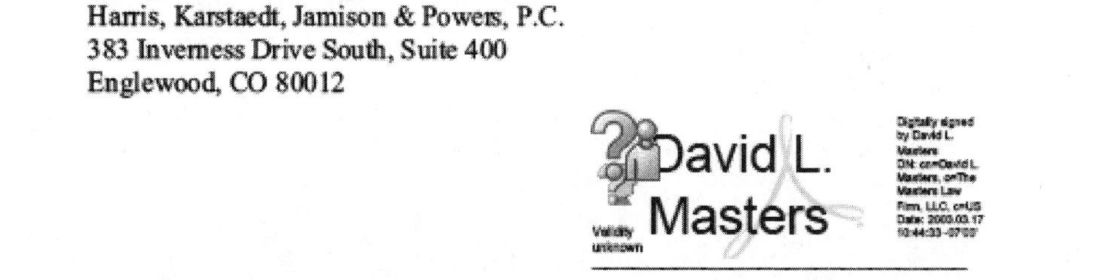

CERTIFICATE OF SERVICE

The undersigned hereby certifies that on the 17th day of March, 2003, a true and correct copy of the foregoing PLAINTIFF'S EIGHTH SUPPLEMENTAL RULE 26(a)(1) DISCLOSURES was served on counsel of record by providing a copy thereof to, and requesting that service be made by, JusticeLink®, to the following:

Jamey W. Jamison, Esq.
Harris, Karstaedt, Jamison & Powers, P.C.
383 Inverness Drive South, Suite 400
Englewood, CO 80012

Figure 8.3

If you routinely digitally sign correspondence sent to clients or opposing counsel, or digitally sign pleadings filed with the courts, you can expect that some recipients of your documents may question the validity of the signature or even reject the document. In contrast, if you use a custom stamp that applies a facsimile of your signature to documents, it will probably go unquestioned. Distributing certificates to validate your digital signature and explaining to the recipients how to save and use the certificate may be all it takes to convince you that a signature stamp is probably no more insecure than your pen-and-ink signature on paper.

§ 8.1.1 Creating an Acrobat Self-Signed Digital ID—Version 6.0

To create a self-signed digital ID file:

> Menu (Create Digital ID): **Advanced** > **Manage Digital IDs** > **My Digital ID Files** > **My Digital ID File** (New Digital ID File)
> Keystroke (Create Digital ID): **Alt+A-I-F-S-N**

The **Create Self-Signed Digital ID** dialog box appears (Figure 8.4). Fill in your identifying information, enter and confirm a password, and click **Create.**

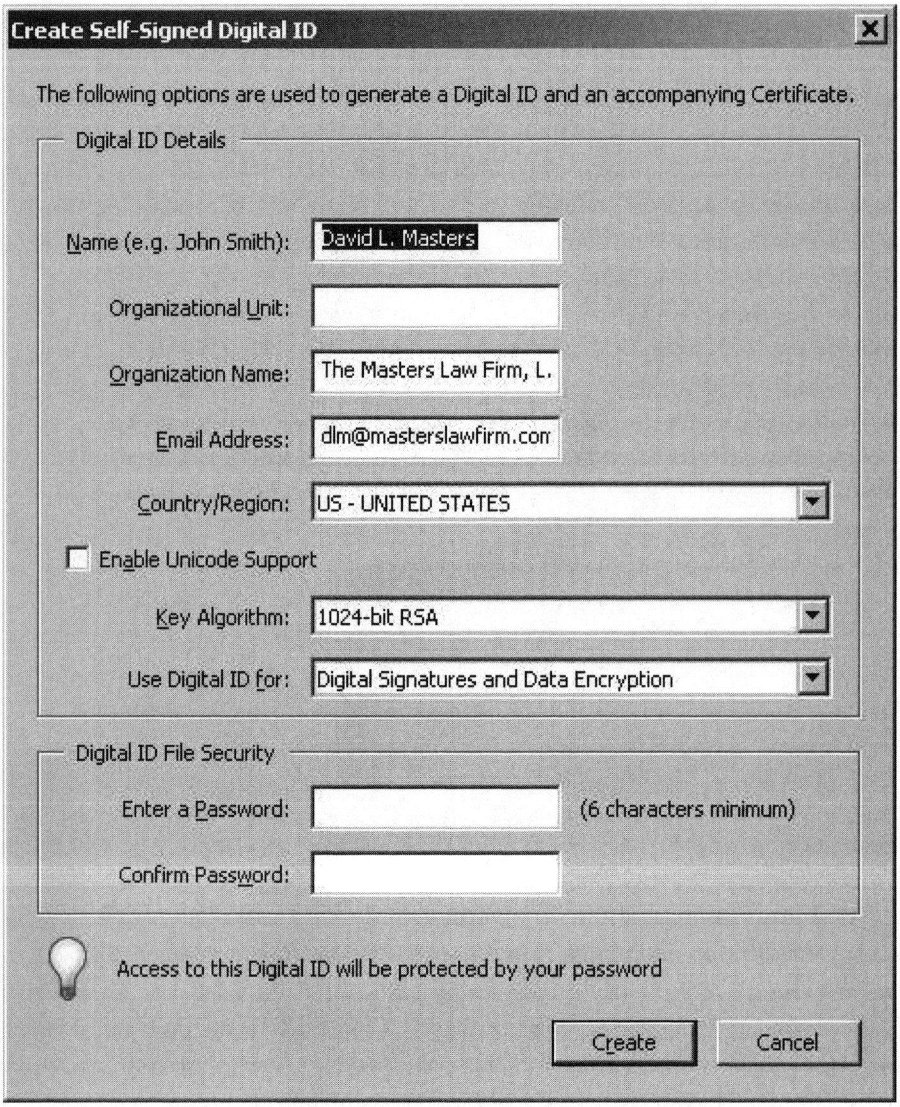

Figure 8.4

§ 8.1.2 Creating an Acrobat Self-Signed Digital ID—Version 7.0

To create a self-signed digital ID file:

> **Menu** (Create Digital ID): Advanced > Security Settings
> **Keyboard** (Create Digital ID): **Alt+A-E**

The Security Settings dialog box appears (see Figure 8.5). Click the button **Add ID**, select **Create a Self-Signed Digital ID**, click **Next** (twice), choose where to store your Self-Signed Digital ID, click **Next**, fill in your identifying information, and click **Finish**.

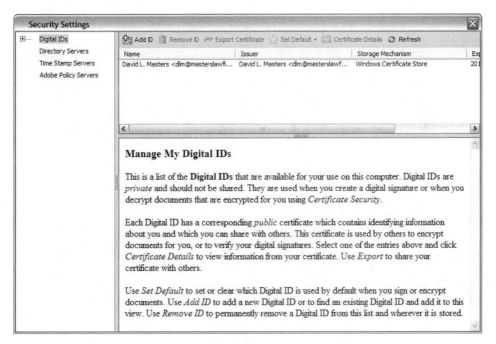

Figure 8.5

§ 8.1.3 Selecting an Acrobat Self-Signed Digital ID

Acrobat 7.0 automatically selects your default digital ID when you start the program and you don't need to go through the process of selecting an ID, unless you have more than one and want to use one other than the default. When you start Acrobat 6.0, your digital ID is not automatically selected. Accordingly, the first time you sign a PDF document after starting Acrobat 6.0, you are required to select a digital ID. If you want to avoid this step, you can select a digital ID after starting Acrobat 6.0. Also, if you use more than one digital ID, then you may want to select the desired ID before signing.

To select an existing self-signed digital ID file:

Menu (Select Digital ID File): **Advanced** > **Manage Digital IDs** > **My Digital ID Files** > **Select My Digital ID**

Keystroke (Select Digital ID File): **Alt+A-I-F-S**

§ 8.1.4 Managing Self-Signed Digital IDs—Version 6.0

To manage the properties and appearance of a self-signed digital ID:

Menu (Manage Digital ID): **Advanced** > **Manage Digital IDs** > **My Digital ID Files** > **My Digital ID File Settings**

If prompted, select the digital ID file, type the password, and click **OK** (Figure 8.6).

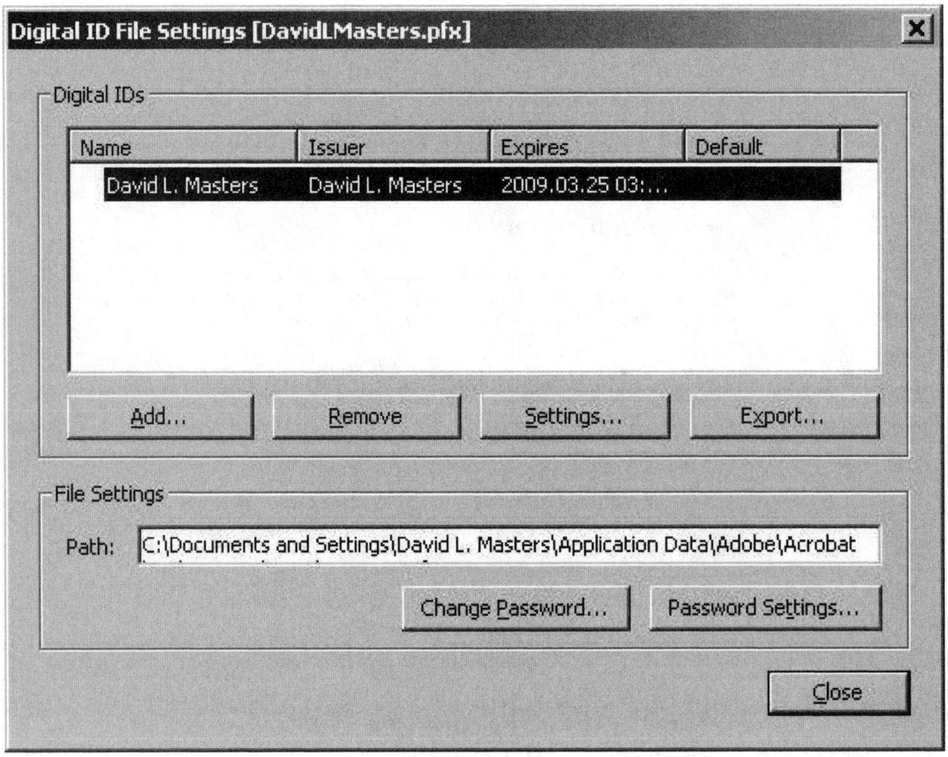

Digital ID File Settings [DavidLMasters.pfx]

Digital IDs

Name	Issuer	Expires	Default
David L. Masters	David L. Masters	2009.03.25 03:...	

Add...   Remove   Settings...   Export...

File Settings

Path: C:\Documents and Settings\David L. Masters\Application Data\Adobe\Acrobat

Change Password...   Password Settings...

Close

Figure 8.6

To change the password, select **Change Password.** Specify the new and old passwords. Passwords are case-sensitive, must contain at least six characters, and may not contain double quotation marks or the following characters: ! @ # $ % ^ & * , | \ ; < > _. Click **OK.**

To change password settings, select the digital ID, choose **Password Settings,** then:

1. To require a password for signing, select **Require Password to Access When Signing.**

2. Select **Always,** or choose a value from the menu to specify how often you are prompted for a password while the digital ID file is selected in the current session.
3. Type your password in the text box.
4. Click **OK.**

When you certify, sign, or validate a document, you can use the Default Certificate Security, the Windows Certificate Security, or a third-party security method. When you install a third-party signature provider, new menu commands may appear. Use these commands instead of, or in addition to, the Manage Digital IDs commands. In addition, a Third-Party Preferences submenu may appear on the Edit menu so that you can change the provider's preference settings.

§ 8.1.5 Managing Self-Signed Digital IDs—Version 7.0

Managing the properties and appearance of a Self-Signed Digital ID takes place in two different locations in Acrobat 7.0. Your digital ID is managed in Security Settings while the appearance of your signature is managed in Preferences—Security. Management of your digital IDs in Security Settings allows for the addition, removal, export, set as default and viewing of certificate details. To manage Digital ID certificates:

Menu (Manage Digital ID): **Advanced > Security Settings**

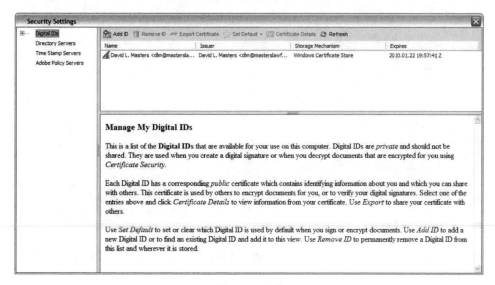

Figure 8.7

Keystroke (Manage Digital ID): **Alt+A-E**

To manage the appearance of a Self-Signed Digital ID go to preferences.

Menu (Configure Signature Appearance): **Edit > Preferences** [select **Security** in the left pane]

Keystroke (Configure Signature Appearance): **Alt+E-N**

or

Keystroke (Configure Signature Appearance): **Ctrl+K**

From the Preferences dialog box with Security highlighted in the left-pane click New to configure a new digital signature or Edit to modify the properties of an existing digital signature. The Configure Signature Appearance dialog box will appear.

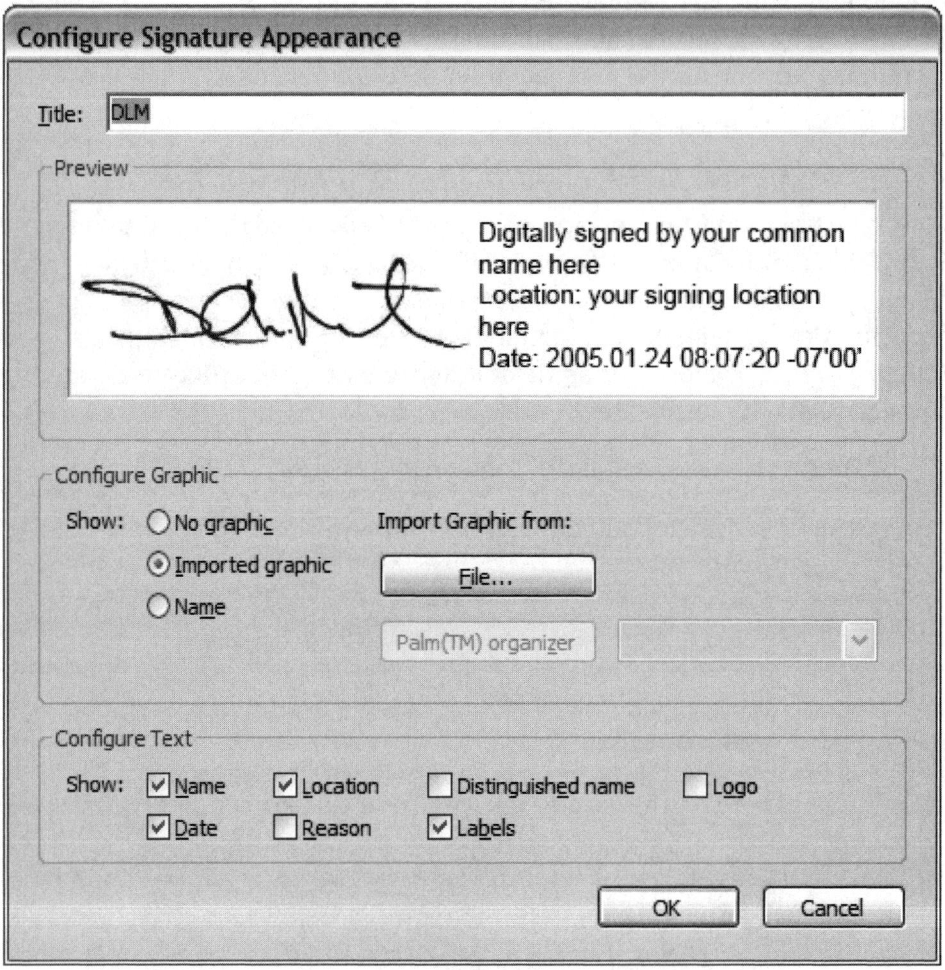

Figure 8.8

The dialog box is divided into two parts: **Configure Graphic** and **Configure Text**. The options are straight-forward. In Configure Graphic you decide whether to include a graphic image with your digital signature. This is where you can specify a scanned copy of your physical signature. In the Configure Text section you decide what text to include with your signature. For example, if you tell Acrobat to display, as part of your digital signature, your name, location, the date and labels and uncheck distinguished name, reason and logo, the result would be as shown in Fig 8.8 (note, this figure also shows that a graphic image of the author's signature was selected to be included in the digital signature).

§ 8.1.6 Specifying a Third-Party Security Method

To install a digital signature from a third-party provider in Version 6.0:

Menu (Specify Third-Party Security): **Edit** > **Preferences,** then click **Digital Signatures**

Keystroke (Specify Third-Party Security): **Ctrl+K**, then click **Digital Signatures**

Choose a provider from the **Default Method to Use When Signing** menu, which lists all security methods installed in the Acrobat Plug-ins folder. If you want to be prompted to select a security method each time you sign, select **Ask When I Sign**, then click **OK.**

To install a digital signature from a third-party provider in Version 7.0:

Menu (Add Third-Party Digital Signature): **Advanced > Security Settings** [click on **Add ID**]

Keystroke (Add Third-Party Digital Signature): Alt+A-E [click on **Add ID**]

The Add Digital ID dialog box appears (see Figure 8.9). Select Get Third-Party ID, click Next and follow the prompts.

§ 8.1.7 Signing a Document with a Self-Signed Digital Signature

To sign a document using an Acrobat self-signed digital signature:

Menu (Signing a Document): **Document** > **Digital Signatures** > **Sign This Document**
    or
Click the **Sign** task button on the toolbar and select **Sign this Document**
    or

1. Click the unsigned signature field in the PDF document.
2. Click **Next** and select **Sign an existing signature field** (if available), create a new one, or create an invisible signature.
3. Click **Next.** If prompted, draw a signature field.
4. In the **Apply Signature to Document** dialog box, type your password if prompted, then click **Sign and Save As** (to sign the document and save it using a different filename) or **Sign and Save** if the document has already been saved with a different filename.

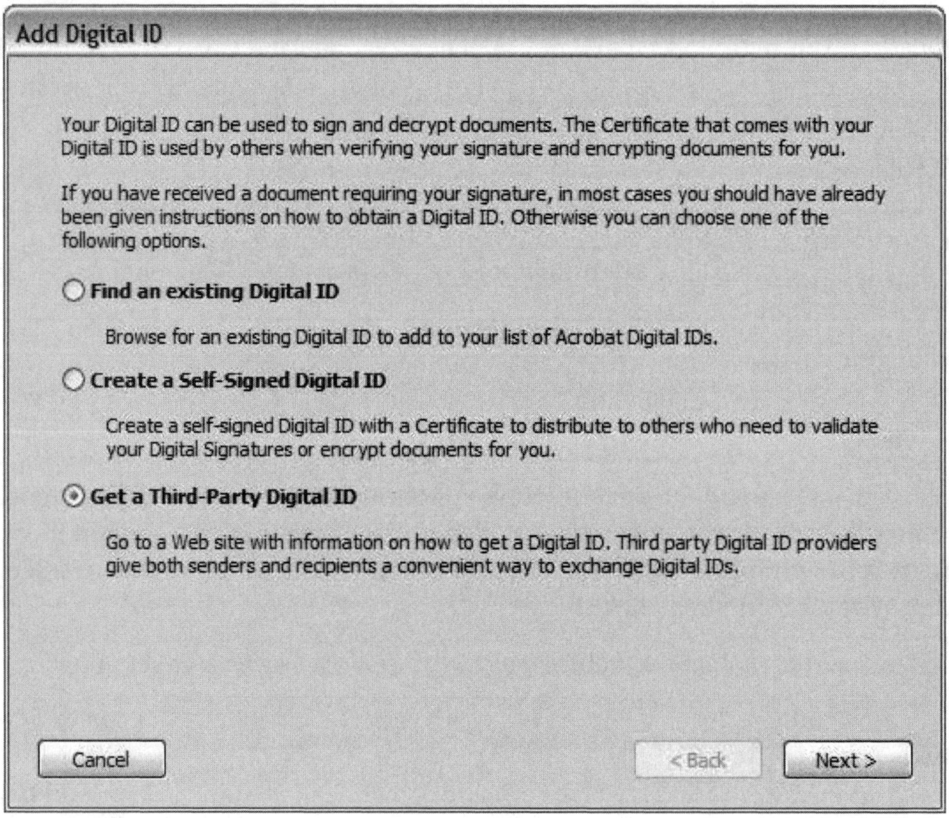

Figure 8.9

Adding a signature does not affect the validity of existing signatures in the document. However, if you make changes to the saved PDF file, you may invalidate the signature. When you sign a document, your signature and the related information can be stored in a signature field embedded on the page. A signature field is an Acrobat form field. You can add a signature field to a page as you sign, or you can use the Signature tool to create an empty signature field that can be signed later. Sign documents only after making final changes. If changes are made to a PDF file after it has been signed, the signature may still be valid, but a caution triangle appears in the signature field and in the Signature tab, indicating that changes were made after the signature was added.

§ 8.2 Validating Someone Else's Signature

When you receive a PDF file signed by another person, you can validate the signature to ensure that the document was indeed signed by that person and hasn't changed after it was signed. In order to validate someone's self-signed digital signature, you must have their certificate. You will obtain their certificate by electronic mail; save the certificate file in a location where you can find it.

Acrobat 6.0 has greatly simplified the process of obtaining a trusted certificate from someone else. To begin the process of obtaining another person's trusted certificate, open the **Manage Trusted Identities** dialog box (Figure 8.10).

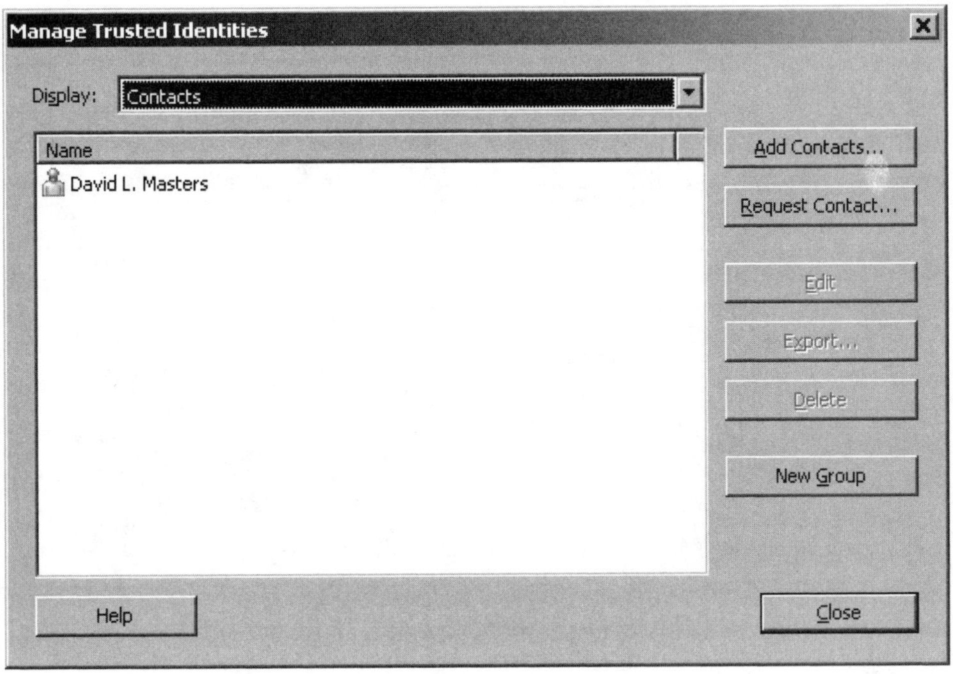

Figure 8.10

6.0 Menu (Manage Trusted Identities): **Advanced** > **Manage Digital Ids** > **Trusted Identities**

6.0 Keystroke (Manage Trusted Identities): **Alt+A-I-T**

7.0 Menu (Manage Trusted Identities): **Advanced** > **Trusted Identities**

7.0 Keystroke (Manage Trusted Identities): **Alt+A-I**

Click on the **Request Contact** button and the **Email a Request** dialog box opens (Figure 8.11).

Fill in or confirm your name, e-mail address, and contact information, then decide whether you want to send your certificate to this person as part of your request for their certificate (check or uncheck the **Include my Certificates** box accordingly).

Click **Next** and select your digital ID to send to the other person (Figure 8.12), click **Select**, then fill in the address of the person to send the e-mail to (the person who you are requesting a trusted certificate from; see Figure 8.13).

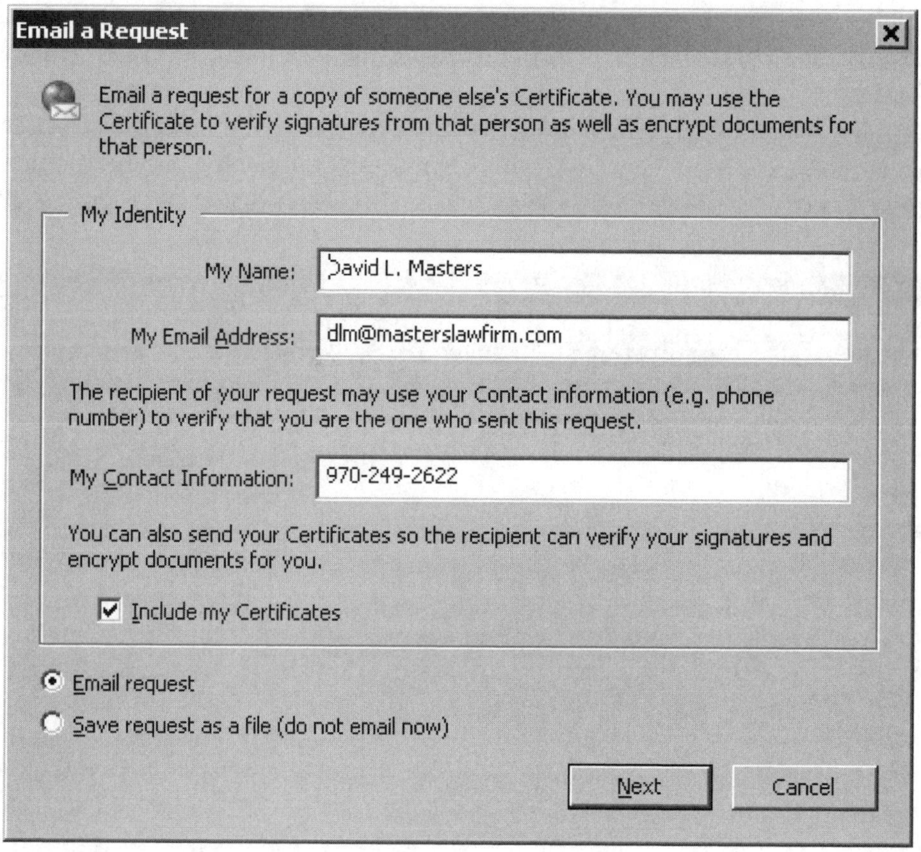

Email a Request ☒

Email a request for a copy of someone else's Certificate. You may use the Certificate to verify signatures from that person as well as encrypt documents for that person.

My Identity

My **N**ame: David L. Masters

My Email **A**ddress: dlm@masterslawfirm.com

The recipient of your request may use your Contact information (e.g. phone number) to verify that you are the one who sent this request.

My **C**ontact Information: 970-249-2622

You can also send your Certificates so the recipient can verify your signatures and encrypt documents for you.

☑ **I**nclude my Certificates

⦿ **E**mail request
○ **S**ave request as a file (do not email now)

[**N**ext] [Cancel]

Figure 8.11

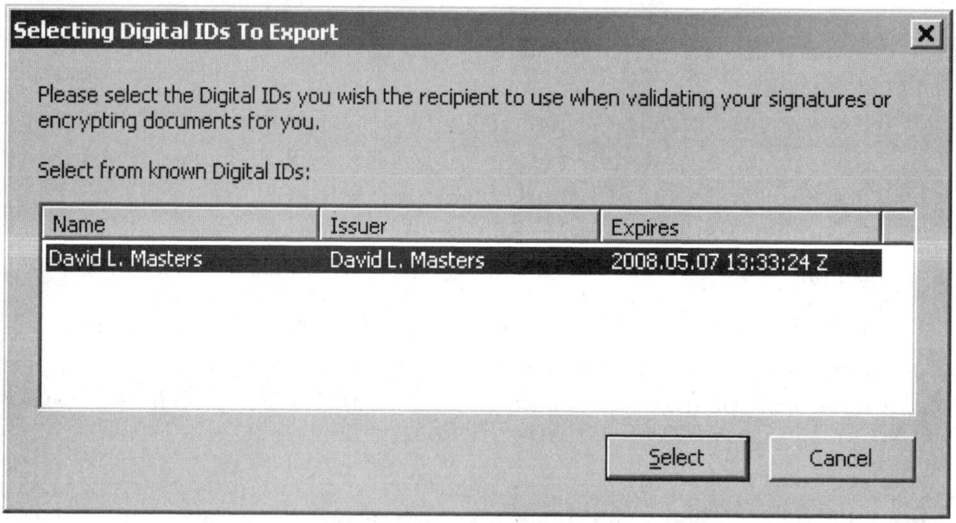

Selecting Digital IDs To Export ☒

Please select the Digital IDs you wish the recipient to use when validating your signatures or encrypting documents for you.

Select from known Digital IDs:

Name	Issuer	Expires
David L. Masters	David L. Masters	2008.05.07 13:33:24 Z

[**S**elect] [Cancel]

Figure 8.12

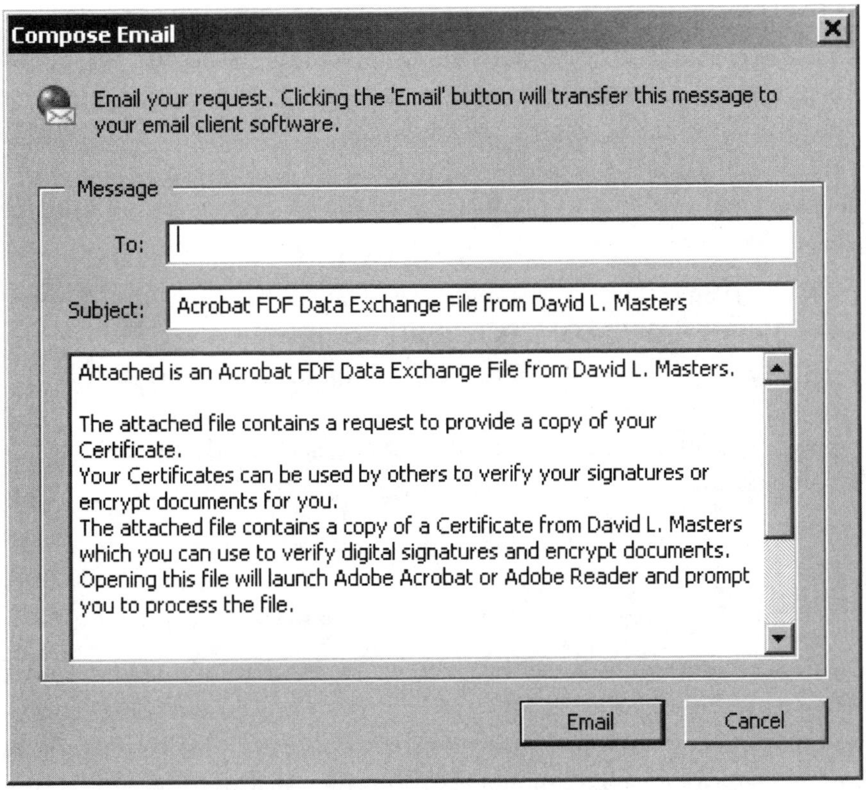

Figure 8.13

Acrobat has composed a message requesting the other person's certificate; clicking on the **Email** button transfers the message to your e-mail client software.

§ 8.2.1 Storing Someone Else's Certificate

To store someone else's self-signed digital signature certificate after you have received it via electronic mail:

6.0 Menu (Storing Someone Else's Signature Certificate): **Advanced > Manage Digital Ids > Trusted Identities**, then click **Add Contacts**)

6.0 Keystroke (Storing Someone Else's Signature Certificate): **Alt+A-I-T**, then click **Add Contacts**

7.0 Menu (Storing Someone Else's Signature Certificate): **Advanced > Trusted Identities,** then click **Add Contacts**)

7.0 Keystroke (Storing Someone Else's Signature Certificate): **Alt+A-I**, then click **Add Contacts**

Click **Browse for Certificates** and navigate to the folder where you store other people's digital signature certificates. Double-click on the file to add it to your trusted contacts list. The certificate needs to be stored and added to the contacts list only one time; after it has been added, the other person's signature can be quickly validated.

§ 8.2.2 Validating the Signature

To validate someone else's signature for whom you have stored a digital signature certificate:

> Menu (Validating Someone Else's Signature): **Document** > **Digital Signatures** > **Validate All Signatures in this Document**
>
> Keystroke (Validating Someone Else's Signature): **Alt+D-D-A**
>
> or
>
> click the **Sign** button on the toolbar and select **Validate All Signatures in this Document**

§ 8.3 Signature Stamps

The Acrobat Stamp feature can be used to create a simple signature stamp. This signature, just like its real-world rubber-stamp counterpart, cannot be verified or secured. However, until we reach a point where courts and opposing counsel require verification of signatures, digital-stamp signatures present a quick and convenient alternative to secure digital signatures.

§ 8.3.1 Creating a Signature Stamp

To create a signature stamp:

1. Sign your name on a piece of paper about a dozen times (or at least until you have created one exemplar that you like enough to use as your Stamp signature).
2. Scan the page of exemplars to PDF (if you want your stamp signature to appear in color [for example, in blue ink], scan in color mode; this increases the size of the stamp file but it's pretty small to start with).
3. Use the **Crop** tool to draw a box around the desired exemplar.
4. Double-click inside the box and click **OK.**
5. Save the resulting PDF document to a convenient location, such as C:\Program Files\Adobe\Acrobat\6.0\Acrobat\Plug_Ins\Annotations\ Stamps\Signatures. You may need to create the Signatures folder; the rest of the path should already exist.
6. Open a PDF document that you want to apply the signature stamp to.
7. In Version 6.0, click on **Tools** > **Commenting** > **Stamp Tool** > **Manage Stamps.** In Version 7.0, click on **Tools** > **Commenting** > **Stamps** > **Manage Stamps**.

8. In the category box, type **Signature**. In the name box, type a name for the stamp (such as your initials).

9. Click **Select** and find where you saved the signature; click **OK**; click **OK** again.

To sign a document with your signature Stamp:

6.0 Menu (Sign Document with Stamp): **Tools** > **Commenting** > **Stamp Tool** > **Signature** and click on your signature stamp.

In Version 7.0, Menu (Sign Document with Stamp): **Tools** > **Commenting** > **Stamps** > **Signatures.**

or, in Version 6.0:

1. Click on the **Stamp Tool** pull-down menu, select the **Signature** category, and click on your signature stamp.

2. Click on the **Stamp** tool.

3. Left-click the document where you want your signature stamp to appear (note: the stamp can be moved, resized, or deleted after it has been applied).

In Version 7.0, click on the **Stamp Tool,** select your signature stamp, then drag it to the desired location on the page.

If you want your signature Stamp to appear at the top of the list of your favorite stamps, in Version 6.0:

Menu: **Tools** > **Commenting** > **Stamp Tool** > **Add Current Stamp to Favorites** for it to show up on top.

If you create a custom stamp for your signature, you'll find it useful for signing documents to be e-mailed or faxed from your computer. If you use the forms feature of Acrobat Professional, you can scan any paper document that needs to be filled in and create form boxes for the areas where information needs to be supplied. When you are done, you simply stamp your signature on the dotted line. Once it is signed, you can fax or e-mail the document from the comfort of your desktop.

§ 8.3.2 Signature Stamp Security

Now that you have created your own digital signature stamp and realize how easy it is to copy or delete that stamp from a PDF file, you should give some thought to securing the document and your signature. In Version 6.0, basic PDF file security can be used to restrict the ability of others to make changes (Figure 8.14). In Version 7.0, apply the desired security policy to the document. For information on using security policies in Acrobat 7.0, see Chapter 11.

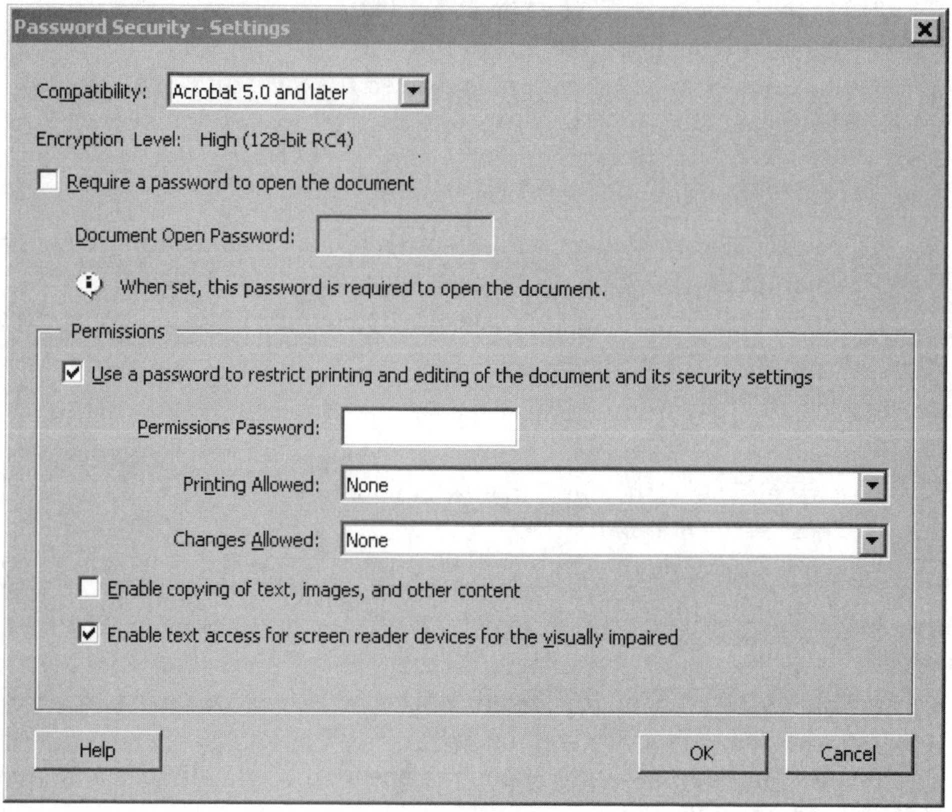

Figure 8.14

In the **Password Security—Settings** dialog box, setting **Changes Allowed** (in the Permissions section) to **None** requires other users to enter the correct password before the document can be changed (including copying or deleting your signature stamp).

Extracting Content from PDF Files

9

The time will come when you want to extract the text from a PDF file to use in another program, typically a word processing application. It may be a set of discovery requests, a contract, or some other document that you have scanned, and now you want to use the text in your own document. When that day comes, there are several options available. The results may not be particularly pretty, but you should be able to extract text from most PDF documents.

Of course text can only be extracted from image-on-text files; image-only files contain no text to extract. If the PDF file that you want to extract text from is an image-only file, it needs to be converted to an image-on-text file using an OCR application. If you use a third-party OCR application, you may be able to generate a text file directly from the PDF document; otherwise the process is to first create an image-on-text PDF file, then extract the text. The first two sections of this chapter discuss methods for extracting text from image-on-text PDF files. The last section covers extracting images. In image-only PDF files the image may look like text, but can only be extracted as a graphic image.

§ 9.1 Using Copy to Extract Text

For short sections of text use the Edit-Copy function:

1. Select the **Select Text** tool (the Select Text tool is located on the basic toolbar) (Figure 9.1).
2. Click and drag to select text.
3. **Ctrl+C** to copy or **Edit** > **Copy.**

Figure 9.1

Switch to the application where you want to use the selected text and use the Windows paste function (**Ctrl+V**) or **Edit** > **Paste.** When the **Single Page** layout is selected (**Preferences** > **Page Display** > **Default Page Layout;** or, by clicking on the **Single Page** icon on the Status Bar), only the text on the current page can be selected. When the **Continuous Page** layout is selected (**Preferences** > **Page Display** > **Default Page Layout;** or, by clicking on the **Continuous Page** icon on the Status Bar), text can be selected over multiple pages.

When the desired text has been selected, use **Ctrl+C** to copy or **Edit** > **Copy,** then switch to the application where you want to use the selected text and use the Windows paste function (**Ctrl+V**) or **Edit** > **Paste.**

Regardless of which method you use to select the text to be copied, be ready to do some editing after you paste it into the other application. This is especially true if the image-on-text PDF file was created by using Paper Capture or a third-party OCR application.

§ 9.2 Extracting Text Using Save As

To extract large amounts of text, such as the text from an entire image-on-text document, use the Save As function to save the file to a text format such as RTF (Rich Text Format—"rich" because it allows for some text formatting such as bold, underline, and italics). To save an image-on-text PDF file as an editable text file:

> Menu (Save As): **File** > **Save As**
> Keystroke (Save As): **Alt+F-A** or **Ctrl+Shift+S**

When the **Save As** dialog box appears, name the file, choose an appropriate location, and then select an editable text format from the **Save as Type** drop-down menu (Rich Text Format works well). See Figure 9.2.

If you use Microsoft Word you can Save As directly to that format. Again, formatting might be an issue. If Save As produces intolerable formatting prob-

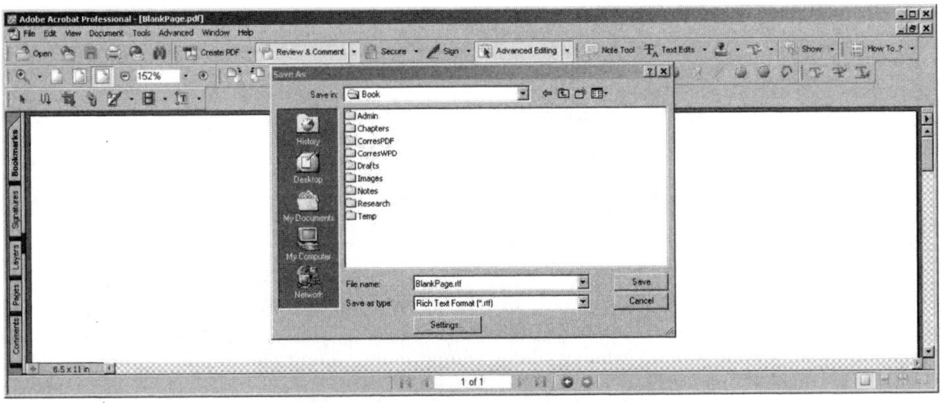

Figure 9.2

lems, select Plain Text (.txt). Saving to plain text format removes all formatting, but sometimes it's easier to add the desired structure than it is to remove unwanted formatting.

§ 9.3 Extracting Graphic Images

Extracting graphics from PDF files might be more useful than you think. You may want to select the graphic image of what looks like a text document if it is important that an exact image of the text be reproduced in another application. For example, you may want to copy the portion of a letter that includes the closing paragraph and author's signature. Then again, there may be no text at all to be captured, such as when you want to paste a portion of a handwritten note into another application (Figure 9.3).

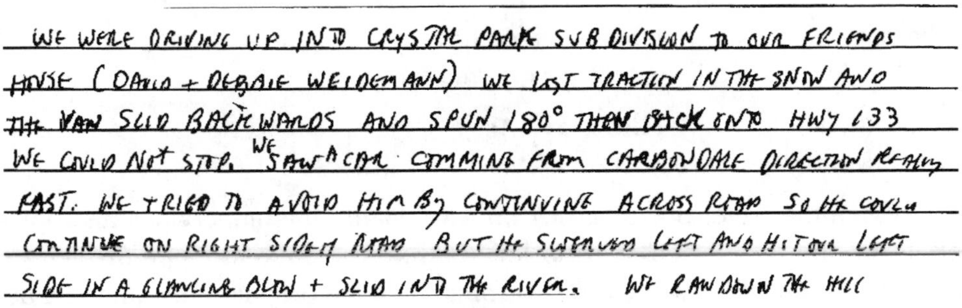
WE WERE DRIVING UP INTO CRYSTAL PARK SUBDIVISION TO OUR FRIENDS HOUSE (DAVID + DEBBIE WEIDEMANN) WE LOST TRACTION IN THE SNOW AND THE VAN SLID BACKWARDS AND SPUN 180° THEN BACK ONTO HWY 133 WE COULD NOT STOP. WE SAW A CAR COMMING FROM CARBONDALE DIRECTION REALLY FAST. WE TRIED TO AVOID HIM BY CONTINUING ACROSS ROAD SO HE COULD CONTINUE ON RIGHT SIDE OF ROAD BUT HE SWERVED LEFT AND HIT OUR LEFT SIDE IN A GLANCING BLOW + SLID INTO THE RIVER. WE RAN DOWN THE HILL

Figure 9.3

Note: the image of the text in an image-on-text file that was created by printing a file to PDF cannot be selected. The image of text in an image-on-text file that was created by OCR can be selected, copied, and pasted.

§ 9.3.1 Using Copy to Extract Images

To select and copy an image:

1. Select the **Select Image** tool (Figure 9.4).

Figure 9.4

2. Click and drag to draw a box around the desired image or portion of an image.
3. Use **Ctrl+C** to copy or **Edit** > **Copy.**

Switch to the application where you want to use the selected image and use the Windows paste function (**Ctrl+V**) or **Edit** > **Paste.** The selected portion of the PDF document is pasted into the other application (this assumes that the other application can handle inserting and manipulating graphics.)

In Version 7.0, the Select Tool is by default configured to select text before images so you don't have to tell Acrobat that you want to select an image. The Select Tool can be configured in **Preferences** > **General** > **Selection** to select images before text.

§ 9.3.2 Using Save As to Extract Images

The Save As function may be used to convert an image-only PDF file to another graphic format (such as TIFF or JPEG).

To save a PDF file in another graphic format:

Menu (Save As): **File** > **Save As**
Keystroke (Save As): **Alt+F-A** or **Ctrl+Shift+S**

When the **Save As** dialog box appears, name the file, choose an appropriate location, and then select a format from the **Save as Type** drop-down menu (TIFF and JPEG work well). Acrobat uses the original file name and appends a description of each extracted page using the following format: _Page_0X, where X represents the page number.

§ 9.3.3 Using Export to Extract Images

All images in a PDF file can be exported in a single operation. This may be useful when a PDF file contains several high-quality graphic images. To extract all images from a PDF file:

Menu (Export Images): **Advanced** > **Export all Images**
Keystroke (Export Images): **Alt+A-X**

When the **Export All Images** dialog box appears, navigate to an appropriate location; Acrobat saves each image with a new name in this location. Acrobat uses the original file name and appends a description of each image extracted using the following format: _Page_0X_Image_000Y where X represents the page number and Y represents the sequential number of each image from a particular page. You can use Export All Images to break a multipage image-only PDF file into as many separate image files as there are pages in the document. You can then convert all those image files back to PDF so that you end up with a separate PDF file for each page. If you're wondering why you would ever want to do this, here's one possible scenario. You have a long document that you want to use as an exhibit at trial. However, you expect that the judge or opposing counsel will only allow the use of about half the pages. Rather than extracting the pages that might be allowed, it may be easier to extract all pages as images, and then convert them back to individual PDF files.

Searching and Indexing

10

Now here's something you can't do with paper documents. Okay, sure, you can read through a document looking for particular words, or even read through several documents looking for words or phrases, but you can't do it as fast as your computer can. Searching and indexing are potent features exclusive to digital documents. PDF files, being digital documents, allow for searching and indexing. Image-on-text PDFs are digital documents that can be searched and indexed. Image-only PDFs cannot be searched or indexed; however, comments added to image-only PDFs can be. Searching, finding, and indexing are different functions described in this chapter, but first we need to make sure that we have text that can be found, searched, and indexed.

Lawyers and paralegals often think that because they have a collection of digital documents, those documents can now be searched. Not so fast; remember, not all PDF files are created equal. Image-only documents contain no text; without text there is nothing to search. On the other hand, image-on-text PDF files contain text behind an exact image of the original document. Image-on-text files can be indexed and searched.

The quality of the text behind the image in image-on-text PDF files depends on several factors. In image-on-text PDF files created by scanning and OCR, the quality of the underlying text file depends on the quality of the original scanned document. Large, clean, easily recognizable fonts produce nearly 100 percent accuracy. Small or faint text produces less-accurate results. Documents printed to PDF have exact text behind the image. The results produced can be substantially different; try the experiment in Section 10.2 below. This may seem like a lot of work (it probably takes at least ten minutes), but you will likely learn a lasting and important lesson about OCR.

§ 10.1 Creating Image-on-Text Files

To convert scanned pages (image-only files) to ones with searchable and indexable text (image-on-text files), open an image-only PDF file. Use the Paper Capture feature to OCR an image-only document within Acrobat.

> 6.0 Menu (Paper Capture): **Document** > **Paper Capture** > **Start Capture**
> 6.0 Keystroke (Paper Capture): **Alt+D-U-S**
> 7.0 Menu (Paper Capture): **Document > Recognize Text Using OCR >**
Start
> 7.0 Keystroke (Paper Capture): **Alt+D-Z-S**

The Paper Capture dialog box opens (Figure 10.1). In Version 7.0 it's called the Recognize Text dialog box but otherwise looks the same.

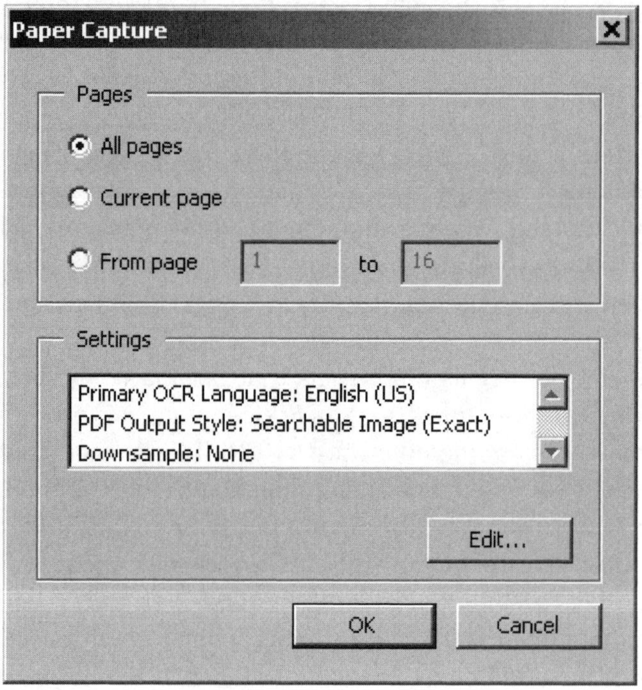

Figure 10.1

Specify the pages to be captured (all, current, or a range of pages), then click **OK** to start the process. Note: if you use StampPDF or IntelliPDF BATES Pro to apply Bates numbers to image-only PDF files, you cannot thereafter use Capture Pages to OCR the content (OmniPagePro 12.0 will OCR stamped image-only PDF files).

§ 10.2 OCR Quality Experiment

1. Open a document in a word processing application.
2. Set the font to a sans serif type (Arian, Universal, and so on), and make it at least 12 points in size.
3. Format the text for double spacing.
4. Print a page or two of this document.

Once you have printed a page or two of this document, scan it to PDF. While you're at it, e-mail it to a colleague and have them print it and fax it back to you. Now take the faxed copy and scan it to PDF (give each file a unique name such as Test1 and Test2). For the next step in the experiment, use the Capture Pages feature in Acrobat or an OCR application that can create image-on-text PDF files. After the two test files have been saved, run each through an OCR application (the following description assumes you do this within Acrobat using the Capture Pages function).

6.0 Menu (Paper Capture): **Document** > **Paper Capture** > **Start Capture**
6.0 Keystroke (Paper Capture): **Alt+D-U-S**
7.0 Menu (Paper Capture): **Document > Recognize Text Using OCR >**
Start
7.0 Keystroke (Paper Capture): **Alt+D-Z-S**

When the OCR (capture) process completes, save and close each file. Now, open the PDF test file that you created by scanning a pristine original, select all of the text on the page (**Ctrl+A**), copy it (**Ctrl+C**), switch to a word processing application (**Alt+Tab**) and paste the text into a new document (**Ctrl+V**). Look at the result for typographical errors that were not present in the original. Now open the PDF test file that was received as a fax, select all of the text on the page (**Ctrl+A**), copy it (**Ctrl+C**), switch to a word processing application (**Alt+Tab**) and paste the text into a new document (**Ctrl+V**). Did you have more typographical errors in the second (scanned) test file? How did it compare to the scanned pristine original? Remember this when you OCR scanned documents with the idea that this will produce a perfect text file that can be searched.

§ 10.3 Searching Image-on-Text PDF Files

Image-on-text can be searched for words or phrases. Use the Search PDF pane to find a word, series of words, or part of a word in the active PDF file or in all PDFs in a particular folder. To search for words in a document, open an image-on-text PDF file:

On the toolbar, click the **Search** tool, or (Figure 10.2)

Figure 10.2

    6.0 Menu (Search): **Edit** > **Search**
    6.0 Keystroke (Search): **Alt+E-S**
or
    6.0 Keystroke (Search): **Ctrl+F**
    7.0 Menu (Search): **Edit** > **Search**
    7.0 Keystroke (Search): **Alt+E-S**
or
    7.0 Keystroke (Search): **Ctrl+Shift+F**

Type the word, words, or part of a word that you want to look for in the space provided in the search pane and click **Search** (Figure 10.3). The results appear in page order, showing a few words of the context in which the search term appears. Click an item from the list to jump to that search result; continue clicking items in the results list, or use the keyboard command **Ctrl+G** to go to the next occurrence in the document.

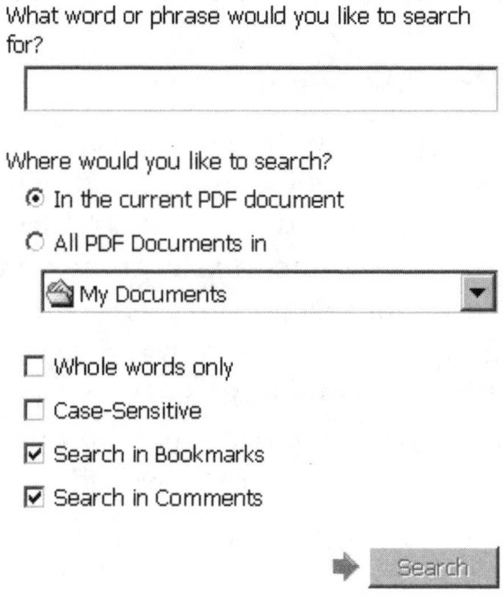

What word or phrase would you like to search for?

Where would you like to search?
    ⊙ In the current PDF document
    ○ All PDF Documents in
    My Documents

    ☐ Whole words only
    ☐ Case-Sensitive
    ☑ Search in Bookmarks
    ☑ Search in Comments

Search

Figure 10.3

§ 10.4 Refining Searches

Searches can be refined by looking for whole words only, making search terms case-sensitive, or by including bookmarks and comments in the text to be searched. You can select any of the following to refine your search:

- **Whole Words Only** finds only occurrences of the complete word you enter in the text box. For example, if you search for the word "legal," the words "illegal" and "legally" are not found.
- **Case-Sensitive** finds only occurrences of the words that are in the case that you typed.
- **Search in Bookmarks** searches the text in the Bookmarks pane as well as the text in the document. Occurrences in the Bookmarks pane appear at the top of the list and are identified with a different symbol than occurrences in the document
- **Search in Comments** searches the text in the comments and in the document text. Instances in the comments text are listed in the search results with a comment icon, the search word, and a word or two of context, and so on. The order in which the occurrences appear is related to their location on the document pages.

§ 10.5 Find—Version 7.0

Acrobat 7.0 returns the simple "find" function found in most Windows applications. When you just want to browse through a document quickly looking for a single word, or, for that matter, any character or string of characters, you issue the command **Ctrl+F**. Many computer users have employed this command for a long time and missed its presence in Acrobat 6.0. Now it's back. To use Find in Acrobat 7.0:

> Menu (Find): **Edit > Find**
> Keystroke (Find): **Alt+E-F**
> or
> Keystroke (Find): **Ctrl+F**

When the command has been issued a small dialog box appears where you type the word or characters to be found (see Figure 10.4). Pressing the Enter key finds the first occurrence; continue to press the Enter key to browse through the document to find each occurrence of the word or characters entered in the find dialog box.

Figure 10.4

§ 10.6 Indexing Using Catalog

In Acrobat Professional, you can use the Catalog feature to create a full-text index of PDF files or document collections (Catalog is not available in Acrobat Standard). This can be helpful if large PDF collections of discovery documents, pleadings or contracts need to be searched repeatedly. Note that information contained in comments and document descriptions related to image-only PDF files are included in the index and found using the Search function. To create an index:

> Menu (Create an Index): **Advanced** > **Catalog** > **New Index**
> Keystroke (Create an Index): **Alt+A-T** and select **New Index**

Type a name for the index, select the folders (directories) that contain the PDF files to be included in the index (you can also select subdirectories to be excluded), and click **Build.**

When you build a new index, the results are a new .pdx file and a new folder (named Index) that contains one or more .idx files. The .pdx file, which is small, makes the information in the .idx files available to the search function. The .idx files contain the index entries that a user finds in the index, so their file sizes—individually or collectively—can be large. All of these files must be available to users who want to search the index. In other words, if you Catalog (index) a large collection of PDF files (documents) and put them on CD-ROM, be sure to include the .pdx file and Index Folder on the disk.

If you use Catalog to index large collections of documents that will be added to from time to time and accessed by multiple users, you should explore the advanced features of this function. For example, you can schedule indexes to automatically update or rebuild. For more information on using Catalog, see the Complete Acrobat 6.0 Help online manual.

> Menu (Help): **Help** > **Complete Acrobat 6.0 Help**
> Keystroke (Help): **Alt+H-H**

The Help manual opens as a separate document. On the Contents tab, select **Searching Adobe PDF Documents,** then select **Cataloging Adobe PDF Collections** (see Figure 10.5).

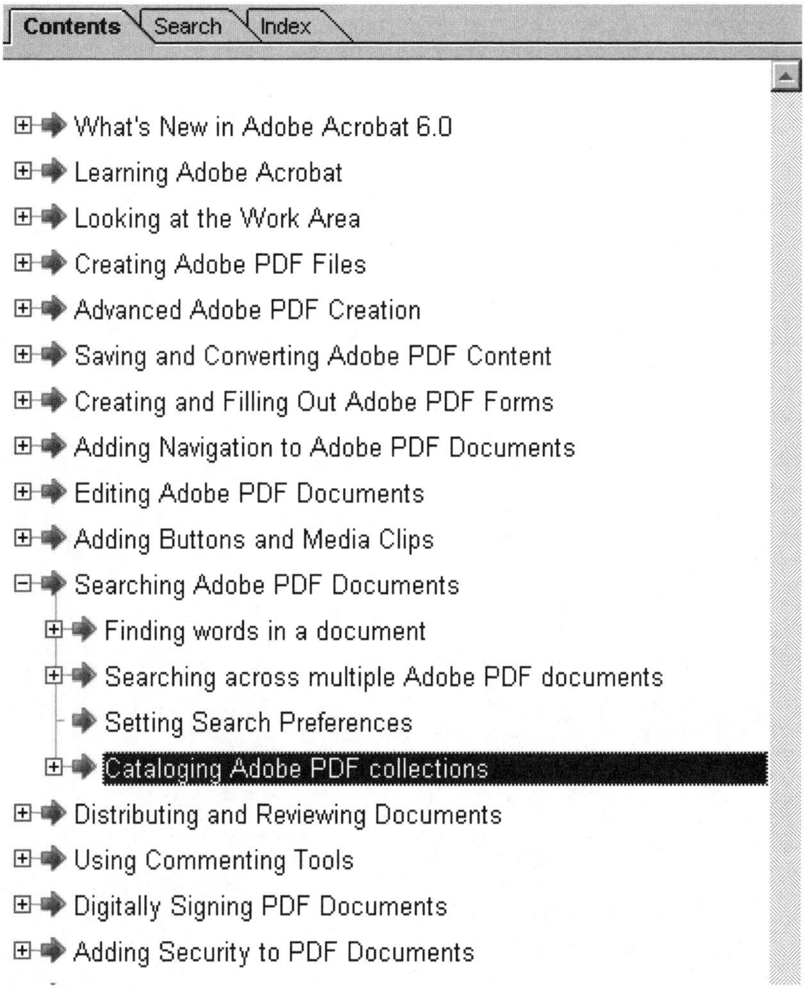

| Contents | Search | Index |

- ⊞➡ What's New in Adobe Acrobat 6.0
- ⊞➡ Learning Adobe Acrobat
- ⊞➡ Looking at the Work Area
- ⊞➡ Creating Adobe PDF Files
- ⊞➡ Advanced Adobe PDF Creation
- ⊞➡ Saving and Converting Adobe PDF Content
- ⊞➡ Creating and Filling Out Adobe PDF Forms
- ⊞➡ Adding Navigation to Adobe PDF Documents
- ⊞➡ Editing Adobe PDF Documents
- ⊞➡ Adding Buttons and Media Clips
- ⊟➡ Searching Adobe PDF Documents
  - ⊞➡ Finding words in a document
  - ⊞➡ Searching across multiple Adobe PDF documents
  - ➡ Setting Search Preferences
  - ⊞➡ Cataloging Adobe PDF collections
- ⊞➡ Distributing and Reviewing Documents
- ⊞➡ Using Commenting Tools
- ⊞➡ Digitally Signing PDF Documents
- ⊞➡ Adding Security to PDF Documents

Figure 10.5

Document Security 11

Acrobat provides a level of security for PDF files not available for documents created and shared in their original word processing format. If you worry about the meta data that accompanies word processing files that you share with opposing counsel, Acrobat provides relief. Printing a word processing document to PDF removes all meta data, at least for now. As software developers (Adobe and Microsoft included) work to integrate products, it could be that meta data will be included in files converted from one format to another.

But there is more to document security than just meta data. For example, PDF files can be set to prevent viewers from selecting text or printing. This can be useful when sending documents to clients for review if you are concerned about sharing your work product before you have been paid. If you're really paranoid, you can set security so that PDF files can only be opened by persons with Trusted Certificates. Both basic security and certificate security use 128-bit encryption (strong stuff).

§ 11.1 Basic PDF Security—Version 6.0

Basic PDF security allows you to require a password to open a document or require a password to perform certain editing functions (change, print, or select text). To set basic security rights:

Toolbar (Document Security): Click on the **Secure** icon on the main toolbar and select **Restrict Opening and Editing** (see Figure 11.1)

Figure 11.1

Menu (Document Security): **Document > Security > Restrict Opening and Editing**

Keystroke (Document Security): **Alt+D-Y-R**

The **Password Security—Settings** dialog box appears (Figure 11.2).

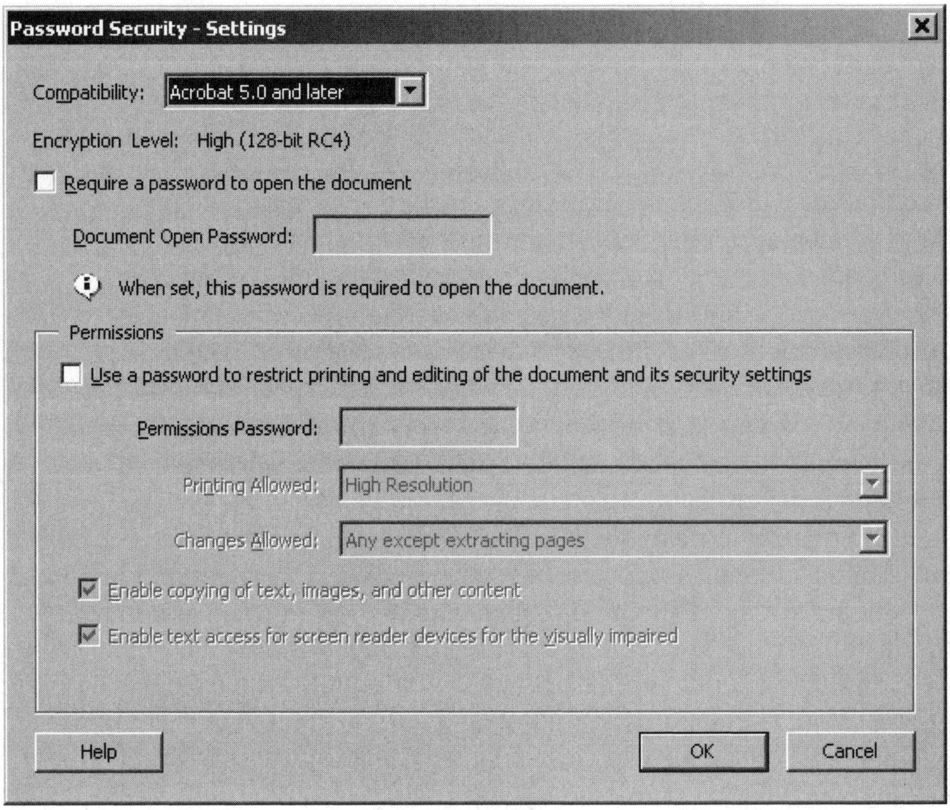

Figure 11.2

You can specify and require a password to open the document or to permit printing, editing, and copying of text.

To require a password to open the document, check the box and type a password. To require a password to restrict printing and editing, check the box and type a permissions password. By default, once you restrict editing, users are not able to select and copy content from the document (text and graphics). To allow users to select and copy content from the document, check the appropriate box.

§ 11.2 PDF Security—Version 7.0

Before you can secure a document in Version 7.0, you need to select a Security Policy to apply to the document. Acrobat 7.0 ships with five existing security policies. You can copy or edit the existing policies, or create your own. Basic PDF security comes from applying the "Restrict Opening and Editing Using Passwords . . ." policy. Now that's a long name; so here's a policy that you could edit and simply rename as "Password Protect" (or some other short and simple name). This policy allows you to require a password to open a document or require a password to perform certain editing functions (change, print or select text). Before we apply the password policy that ships in Acrobat 7.0, we need to set it up the way we want. You can do this with any of the policies. In the example below, we take the policy "Restrict Opening and Editing Using Passwords . . ." and rename it "Password to Edit-Copy-Print," then set up a security policy that does just that—requires a password to edit, copy, or print the document—anyone can open it but will need the password to do more. To edit the security policy:

Toolbar (Document Security): Click on the **Secure** icon on the main toolbar and select **Manage Security Policies**

Menu (Document Security): **Document > Security > Manage Security Policies**

Keyboard (Document Security): **Alt+D-C-M**

The **Managing Security Policies** dialog box will appear (see Figure 11.3). Next, highlight the policy "Restrict Opening and Editing Using Passwords . . ." and click **Copy** (you could edit, but it's safer to copy and save with a new name). The **Creating a new Security Policy from an existing Security Policy** dialog box appears (see Figure 11.4). Change the policy name to "Password to Edit-Copy-Print" and check the check box to "Save passwords with policy." (See Figure 11.4.) Now click **Next** to continue the process and a new dialog box (with the same name as the last) appears (see Figure 11.5). In the Permissions section, enter a password, leave the "Printing allowed" selection at None, leave the "Changes allowed" selection at None (or choose one from the drop-down list), and leave unchecked the box to "Enable copying of text, images, and other contents." Click **Next**, confirm the password, click **OK**, then **Finish**.

The next time you want to apply this policy to require a password for users to edit, copy, or print the document:

Toolbar (Secure Document): Click on the **Secure** icon on the Toolbar, select **Secure this Document,** highlight the policy and click **Apply**;

Menu (Secure Document): **Document > Security > Secure this Document,** highlight the policy and click **Apply**; or

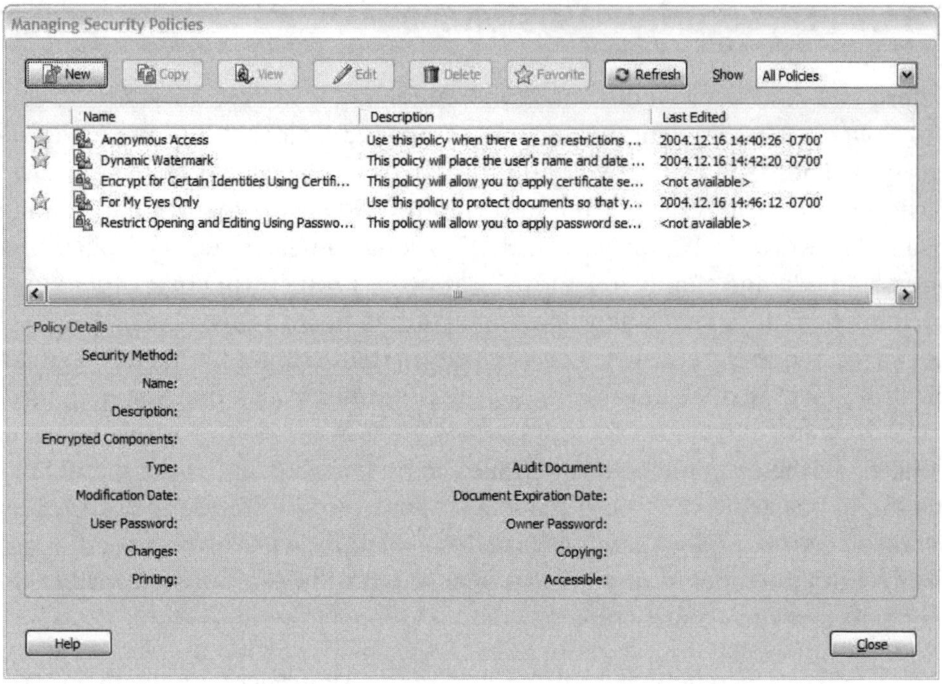

Figure 11.3

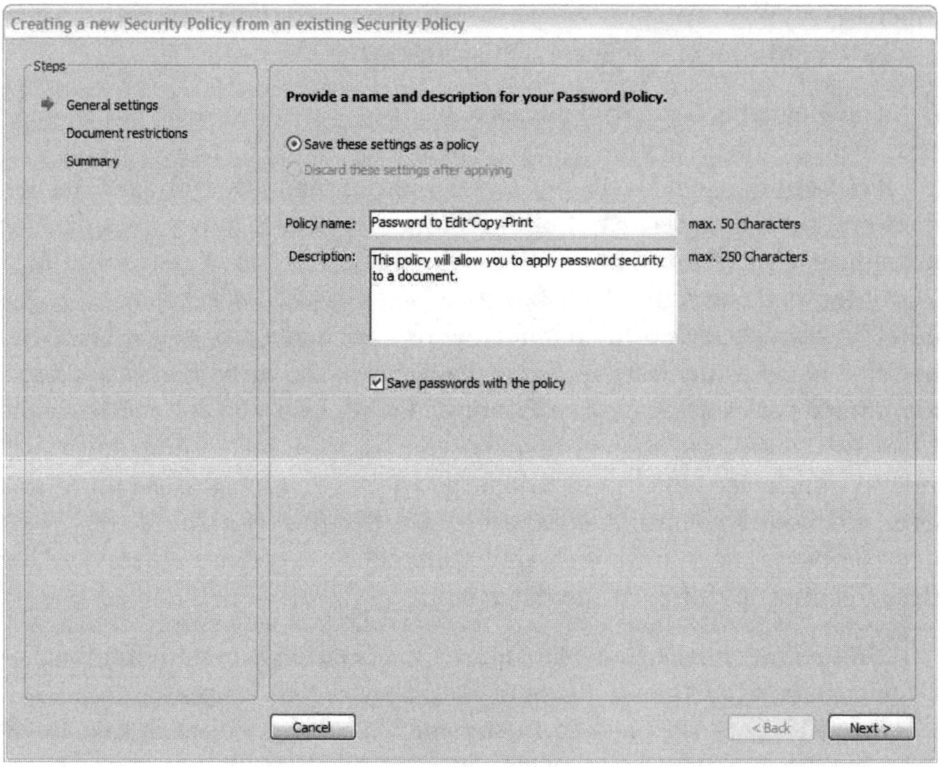

Figure 11.4

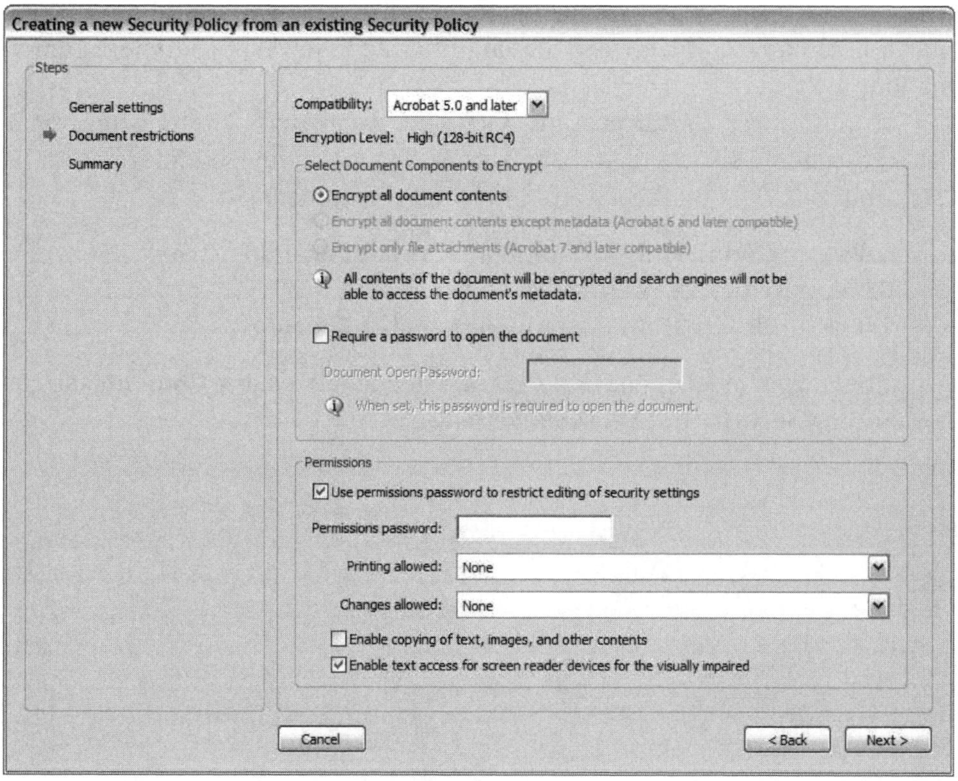

Creating a new Security Policy from an existing Security Policy

Steps

    General settings

➡ Document restrictions

    Summary

Compatibility: [Acrobat 5.0 and later ▾]

Encryption Level: High (128-bit RC4)

Select Document Components to Encrypt

    ◉ Encrypt all document contents

    ○ Encrypt all document contents except metadata (Acrobat 6 and later compatible)

    ○ Encrypt only file attachments (Acrobat 7 and later compatible)

    ⓘ All contents of the document will be encrypted and search engines will not be able to access the document's metadata.

☐ Require a password to open the document

    Document Open Password: [   ]

    ⓘ When set, this password is required to open the document.

Permissions

    ☑ Use permissions password to restrict editing of security settings

    Permissions password: [   ]

    Printing allowed: [None ▾]

    Changes allowed: [None ▾]

    ☐ Enable copying of text, images, and other contents

    ☑ Enable text access for screen reader devices for the visually impaired

[Cancel]   [< Back] [Next >]

Figure 11.5

Keystroke (Secure Document): **Alt+D-C-S,** highlight the policy and click **Apply**.

Remember that you can create new, copy, or edit security policies to make them suit your particular needs. If you want to send documents to a prospective client who has not yet signed your fee agreement and given a retainer, for example a lease or draft articles of incorporation, then you may want to let the client prospect view the documents on their computer but not allow them to print your work product (and file it on their own without ever calling you again).

§ 11.3 Advanced (Certificate) PDF Security

You can restrict PDF files so that they can only be opened by selected users. To select those users, you must have their digital identification certificate so that their identity can be associated with the document. If you plan to use this feature, it might be worthwhile to create a folder on your local hard disk drive for storing certificates (such as C:\TrustedCertificates). Each person who has rights in the document must send you a certificate so that you can associate his or her identity with a specific document. This might be useful when working with co-counsel to prevent the unauthorized viewing of privileged information.

Using Trusted Certificates for document security is akin to using certificates to validate secure digital signatures. For more detailed information on this topic, see the Complete Acrobat 6.0 Help document.

6.0 Menu (Help): **Help** > **Complete Acrobat 6.0 Help**
6.0 Keystroke (Help): **Alt+H-H**
7.0 Menu (Help): **Help** > **Complete Acrobat 7.0 Help**

The Help manual opens as a separate document. On the **Contents** tab, select **Adding Security to PDF Documents.**

Saving Web Pages to PDF 12

With Acrobat installed, you can convert any printable file displayed on your computer to PDF, including Web pages. But Acrobat goes one better by allowing you to create PDF documents from Web pages. Whether generated by printing or creating, PDF files derived from Web pages are image-on-text files. Printing a Web page to PDF is a simple function that produces an image-on-text file of the page displayed. Creating a PDF file from a Web page, on the other hand, captures much more information, including links and imbedded media files (audio, video, flash, and so on). When creating a PDF file from a Web page, you decide how many levels to capture (this feature was called Web Capture in prior versions of Acrobat). PDF files created from Web pages can include active links from the pages, depending on the number of levels captured (Get Only *n* Levels). If the linked pages are not included in the PDF, Acrobat prompts the user to open the pages in a browser (in other words, connect to the Internet and open the page in your default browser).

Why would you want to create a multilevel PDF file from a Web page? Consider municipal codes, county regulations, court rules, and the like. Often, these primary source materials are available online and you may want to have them available when no Internet connection exists, or you may want to include them on a CD-ROM to be delivered to a court or client. Indeed, the CD-ROM option can be particularly useful as these files are often quite large. The Federal Rules of Civil Procedure, created with the levels-to-capture set to two, initially produced a 267-page PDF file that was 1.4 megabytes (MB).

Creating PDFs from Web pages produces a static image of the pages captured. This can be helpful in litigation where expert witnesses may have materials posted on a Web site. You can capture those materials as they exist at
a point in time; if the expert later changes the content, you have an exact copy
of what was previously posted.

§ 12.1 Creating PDFs from Web Pages

Like most tasks in Acrobat, you can create a PDF from Web pages in several
ways.

Toolbar (Create PDF from Web Page): Click on the **Create PDF** button
on the main toolbar and select **From Web Page** (Figure 12.1)

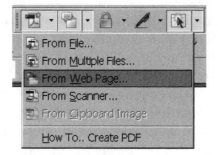

Figure 12.1

Menu (Create PDF from Web Page): **File** > **Create PDF** > **From Web
Page**
Keystroke (Create PDF from Web Page): **Alt+F-F-W**
or
Keystroke (Create PDF from Web Page): **Ctrl+Shift+O**

Version 7.0 offers yet another option for creating a PDF from a Web page.
A tool has been added to the File Toolbar specifically for this purpose. Just
click on the **Create PDF from Web Page Tool** (see Figure 12.2). Regardless of
the method employed or the version used, the Create PDF from Web Page
opens (see Figure 12.3).

Figure 12.2

Then do the following:

1. Type (or easier, paste) the URL of the Web site.
2. Select the number of levels to capture or select **Get entire site.**
3. Click **Create.**

Now sit back and wait for the amount of information selected to be down-loaded to your computer and converted to PDF format. Depending on the amount of information selected and the speed of your Internet connection, this may take a short time or long time. The Federal Rules (267 pages, 1.4 MB) took approximately fifteen minutes over a 500+ KB connection.

§ 12.2 Web Page Capture Settings

Okay, so that's the basics of creating PDFs from Web pages. This is a very pow-erful feature with many custom settings available that deserve attention. So let's go back to the **Create PDF from Web Page** dialog box (see Figure 12.3 above), and click on the **Settings** button (Figure 12.4).

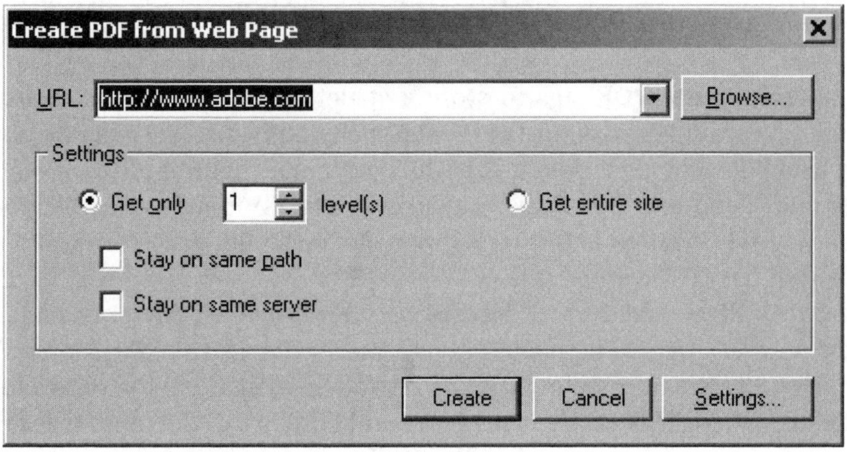

Figure 12.3

First, notice the two tabs: General and Page Layout.

§ 12.2.1 General Settings

In the **General** tab of the **Web Page Conversion Settings** dialog box, check **Create bookmarks** to create a tagged bookmark for each converted Web page, using the page title (taken from the HTML title element) as the bookmark name. If the page has no title, the URL is used as the bookmark name.

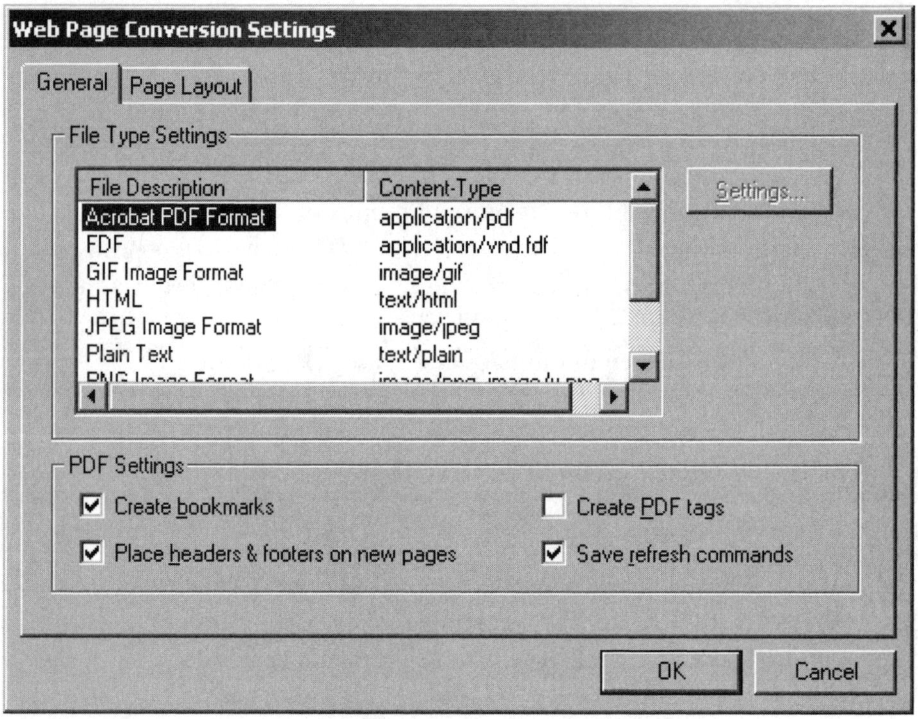

Figure 12.4

Check **Create PDF tags** to store a structure in the PDF file that corresponds to the HTML structure of the original Web pages. This can be particularly useful for complex documents that contain structure information (such as a table of contents, headings, and so on). If this option is selected, you can create tagged bookmarks for paragraphs, list elements, table cells, and other items that use HTML elements.

Check **Place headers & footers on new pages** to place a header and footer on every page. The header shows the Web page title; the footer shows the page URL, the page number in the downloaded set, and the date and time of the download. This can be useful for "authenticating" documents for use in litigation.

Check **Save refresh commands** to save a list of all URLs and remember how they were downloaded in the PDF file for the purpose of refreshing (updating) pages. This option must be selected before you can update a PDF-converted Web site.

For **File Type Settings,** select the file type to be downloaded. If you select **HTML** (see more HTML options below) or **Plain Text** as the file type, you can control the font properties and other display characteristics.

§ 12.2.2 Page Layout Settings

In the **Web Page Conversion Settings** dialog box, click the **Page Layout** tab, and select a page size or enter a custom page width and height in the boxes below the page size menu. Then specify the page orientation and margins. Select the scaling options:

- ◆ **Scale wide contents to fit page** rescales a page's contents, if necessary, to fit the width of the page. If you do not select this option, the paper size is adjusted to fit the page's contents as necessary.

- ◆ **Switch to landscape if scaled smaller than** changes the orientation of the page from portrait to landscape if the contents of a page are scaled beyond a specified percentage. If the PDF version will be less than 70 percent (the default setting) of the original size, the display switches to landscape. This option is available only if portrait orientation has been selected (if landscape orientation was selected, then all pages are captured in landscape orientation).

§ 12.2.3 Additional HTML Capture Settings

In the **General** tab of the **Web Page Conversion Settings** dialog box, double-click **HTML,** or select **HTML** and click **Settings.** In the **General** tab, select from the following options:

- ◆ **Default Colors** sets the default colors for text, page backgrounds, links, and text that replace an image in a file when the image is unavailable. For each color, click the color button to open a palette, and select the color. To use these colors on all pages, select **Force These Settings for All Pages.** If you do not select this option, your color choices are used only on pages that do not have colors defined.

- ◆ **Background Options** specify whether to display colors and tiled images in page backgrounds and colors in table cells. If you do not select these options, converted pages may look different than they do in the Web browser, but they may be easier to read if printed.

- ◆ **Wrap Lines Inside PREs Longer Than** wraps preformatted (HTML) lines of text if they are longer than a specified length. The Web page is scaled so the longest line on the page fits on the screen. Select this setting if an HTML file you're downloading has unreasonably long lines of preformatted text.

- ◆ **Multimedia** options determine whether to reference multimedia (such as .swf files) by URL, disable multimedia capture, or embed multimedia files when possible.

- ◆ **Convert Images** includes images in the conversion to PDF. If you do not select this option, an image is indicated by a colored border (and possibly text, if specified by page design).

- ◆ **Underline Links** underlines textual links on the pages.

The **Fonts and Encoding** tab provides options that are not likely to be needed in the average law office.

Plug-ins | 13

Plug-ins; now here's something that might be difficult or at least intimidating for those who don't regularly dig into their software. But plug-ins are easy enough to understand; they are software modules that add capabilities to Acrobat, allowing you to be more productive. Web browsers have long used plug-ins to add functionality, but we can go back farther than that. Think of the macros that you have written or acquired and then saved in a specific folder so that your word processing application could perform additional tasks (like formatting and printing envelopes). Plug-ins are to Acrobat as macros are to word processing applications. But, you ask, what can plug-ins do that Acrobat can't already? Granted, many plug-ins are intended for document production houses, not law firms. But there are, among the hundreds of available plug-ins, those that fit perfectly in the law office.

If you are at all curious about plug-ins, visit one or more of the following Web sites:

- **www.adobe.com/store**: click on the **plug-ins** link, then select **Adobe Acrobat** from the list of applications
- **www.planetpdf.com**: click on the link for **PDF Tools**
- **www.pdfzone.com**: click on the link for **PDF Toolbox archive**

Plug-ins must be stored in the plug-ins folder in order to load correctly (C:\Program Files\Adobe\Acrobat 6.0\Acrobat\ Plug-Ins). When you buy or download a free plug-in, look for instructions on how to install it to the proper folder.

123

There are plug-ins for building better PDF forms, for managing documents and collections of documents, for enhancing links and bookmarks, and just about anything else you can imagine. Plug-ins for Bates numbering and for redacting confidential or privileged information are almost essential for lawyers.

§ 13.1 Bates Numbering

Bates numbering, or Bates stamping, refers to numbering each page of a document with a unique number. Bates numbers allow lawyers to keep track of all documents produced or received during the course of litigation. The numbers increase by one digit on each page and used to be applied to paper documents using a hand-stamp machine originally manufactured by the Bates Manufacturing Company. The machines were prone to errors (if, for example, the operator turned two pages instead of one) and were messy to work with (the stamp elements were metal and required regular applications of ink). Asking a staff person to Bates number a stack of documents almost guaranteed receiving a dirty look.

Macros for both Word and WordPerfect generate Bates-number labels. Using a macro to create Bates-number labels allows lawyers to prefix the numbers with an alpha code (resulting in a number such as "DLM000001"). Bates-number labels work best on clear return-address labels because they are small (eighty per page). However, the labels come at a price, and applying a label to each page is, to say the least, labor intensive (not to mention the opportunity for errors to occur).

PDF files can be Bates numbered using a plug-in built for that purpose. Using a Bates numbering plug-in is fast, clean, and 100 percent accurate. A thousand pages can be Bates numbered in less than five minutes. No pages are skipped and no one gets indelible ink on their hands. The two most popular Bates numbering plug-ins are discussed below. Note: if you use StampPDF or IntelliPDF BATES PRO to apply Bates numbers to image-only PDF files, you cannot thereafter use Capture Pages to OCR the content (OmniPagePro 12.0 will OCR stamped image-only PDF files). If you want the ability to search Bates-numbered documents, perform Capture Pages before applying the numbers.

§ 13.2 StampPDF (Bates Numbering Plug-in)

StampPDF by Appligent (**www.appligent.com**) allows users to easily include the date, time, contact information, page numbers, watermarks, disclaimers, or any text in any font in any color. Moreover, one specific feature of StampPDF recommends this plug-in for any lawyer using Acrobat in the context of litigation: Bates numbering. The StampPDF plug-in lets you add permanent text or images to any PDF document by just choosing a menu item within Acrobat—no need to launch a separate application. Text may be added diagonally across a document as watermarks ("Draft" or "Confidential," for example), or as headers or footers. Text stamps may be made in a variety of fonts and text styles, including color. Information stamped into the PDF document becomes part of the document and is present when it is displayed and printed. You can specify text size, font, justification, top or bottom placement, diagonal orientation, and whether text is printed on top of or underneath the existing PDF document contents. Text can be stamped in black, white, any shade of gray, or any RGB color. Formatting choices can be saved in a template file for use with other PDF documents to automate the stamping process.

Stamping is done by entering text and formatting choices in a dialog box that appears when you select a StampPDF command from the Acrobat Document menu.

Menu (StampPDF): **Document** > **Single Stamp. . .**
(No keyboard command)
The **Stamp Parameters** dialog box opens (Figure 13.1).

§ 13.2.1 Setting the Beginning Bates Number

Bates numbering with StampPDF is fast and efficient. The plug-in allows numbers in the format of six characters (for example, 000001 for page 1). The Stamp Parameter dialog includes Bates Number in the drop-down list of codes. It lets you begin Bates numbering with the number and page you specify (if you don't specify a beginning number, then the first page is stamped 000001). For example, you can stamp the start page with 000999, the next page with 001000, and so on. You begin Bates numbering with a specific number by including the number in a variable in this format: **%page numberJ**. For example, **%999J** stamps the first page with 000999, the next page with 001000, and so on. To begin Bates numbering with 999 on the first page in the document being stamped:

1. In the stamp file, enter **1** for the **StartPage** parameter.
2. Enter **%999J** for the **Text** parameter.

You should probably make an easy-to-find note on how to set the Bates starting number, as this is likely to be a task performed just infrequently enough to evade memorization.

§ 13.2.2 Adding Prefixes to Bates Numbers

If you have moved from mechanical Bates numbering machines to labels in order to include prefixes in the Bates number (and to keep your hands clean),

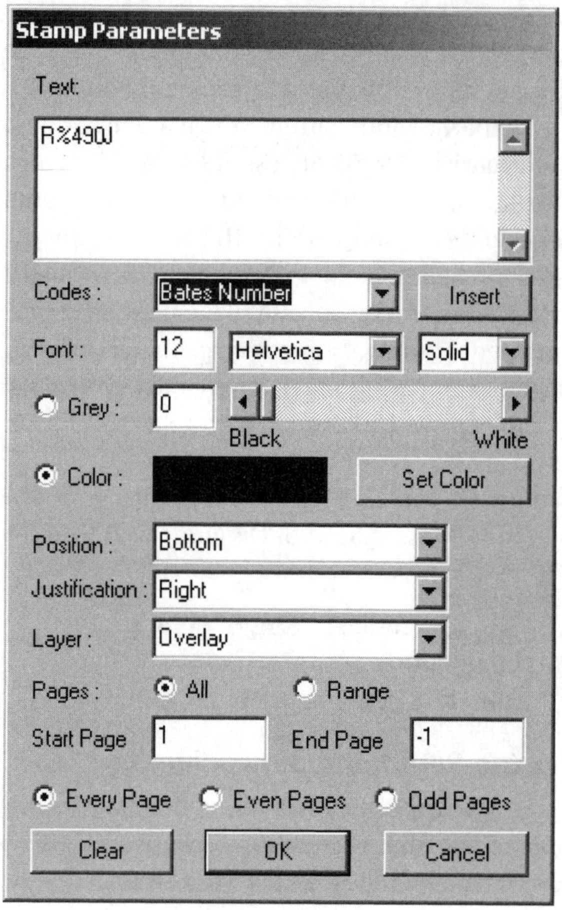

Stamp Parameters

Text:

R%490J

Codes :	Bates Number ▼	Insert
Font :	12 Helvetica ▼	Solid ▼
○ Grey :	0 ◀ ▮	▶
	Black	White
⊙ Color :	■	Set Color
Position :	Bottom ▼	
Justification :	Right ▼	
Layer :	Overlay ▼	
Pages :	⊙ All	○ Range
Start Page	1	End Page -1

⊙ Every Page   ○ Even Pages   ○ Odd Pages

| Clear | OK | Cancel |

Figure 13.1

this feature of StampPDF will be a welcome discovery. Using StampPDF, you can add a prefix to Bates numbers by including the prefix before the variable, such as **ABA%J**. **ABA%J** stamps the first page with ABA000001, the next page with ABA000002, and so on. To include a prefix in the Bates number, simply insert the desired text in front of the Bates numbering variable (the Bates numbering variable is %J). If you want the first page to be ABA000999, then the text in the StampPDF dialog box would look like this: **ABA%999J.**

§ 13.3 IntelliPDF BATES (Bates Numbering Plug-in)

IntelliPDF BATES is a plug-in for Adobe Acrobat that creates and applies custom Bates numbering to PDF files. IntelliPDF BATES can create up to sixteen (thirty-two in the Pro version) stamps per page. Each stamp can consist of up to eight elements (numeric, alphabetical, alphanumeric, roman numerals, and so on) and be up to thirty-two characters long. You control the stamp's creation: the font, size, color, background color, stamp increment, stamp placement, and more. IntelliPDF BATES provides more controls that StampPDF, and as a consequence is slightly more difficult to use. IntelliPDF BATES adds a Plug-Ins menu to the Acrobat menu bar and places a button on the Advanced Editing toolbar (Figure 13.2).

Figure 13.2

It also installs a user's guide that can be accessed from the Help menu.

Menu (IntelliPDF BATES Help): **Help** > **Plug-In Help** > **IntelliPDF BATES**
Keystroke (IntelliPDF BATES Help): **Alt+H-U-I**

§ 13.3.1 Using IntelliPDF BATES

To create and apply Bates stamps using the IntelliPDF BATES plug-in:

Toolbar (IntelliPDF BATES): Click on the **IntelliBATES** button on the Advanced Editing toolbar
Menu (IntelliPDF BATES): **Plug-Ins** > **IntelliPDF Bates**
Keystroke (IntelliPDF BATES): **Alt+P-I**

The **IntelliPDF Bates** dialog box appears, which is divided into five major areas: Bates (upper left), Elements (middle left), Bates Preview (upper-lower left), Advanced Options (lower left), and Full Preview (right). The control buttons are in the lower right (Figure 13.3).

§ 13.3.2 Position, Background, and Pages (Bates Section)

The Bates section of the IntelliPDF Bates dialog box has three tabs for setting the position, background, and pages of each stamp to be applied. Remember, you can apply more than one stamp at a time using IntelliPDF BATES. The Background tab allows you to select a background color for the stamp and adjust the opacity of the background from 0 to 100 percent (transparent to solid).

§ 13.3.3 Properties and Font (Elements Section)

The Elements section of the IntelliPDF BATES dialog box has three tabs for setting the properties and font of the current stamp. Properties refers to the type of Bates stamp (numeric, alphabetical, alphanumeric, numeric-alpha,

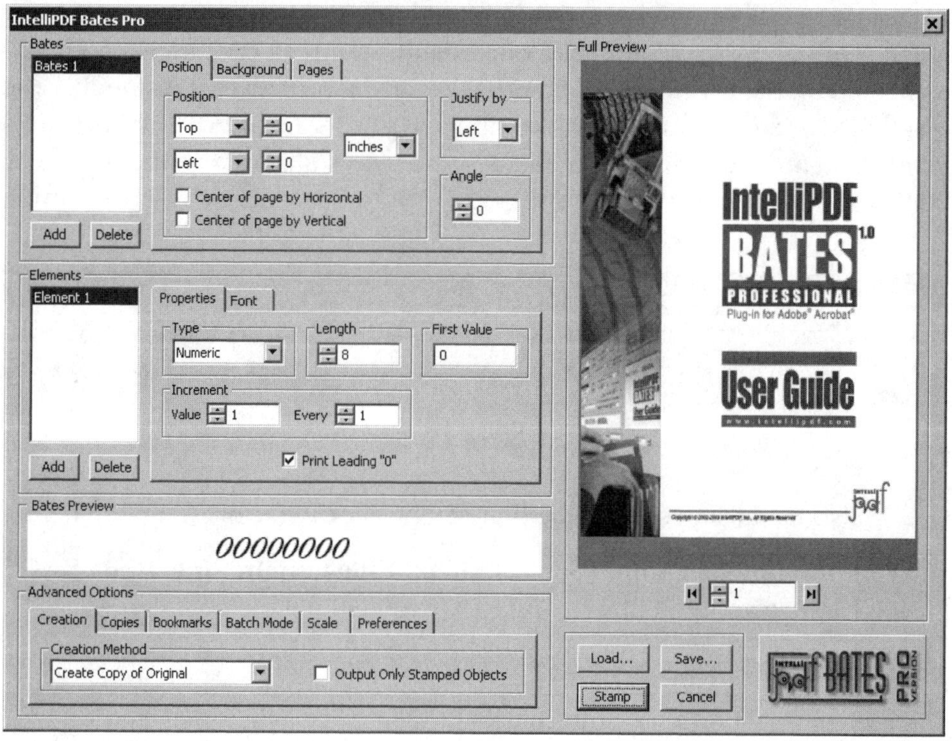

Figure 13.3

static text, or Roman numerals). Properties in the Elements section also lets you control the number of characters in the stamp (length), the beginning value (initial value), and the increment value in terms of how much to increase the stamp and how often (to increase by one every page should be the default).

§ 13.3.4 Preview (Bates Preview Section)

This space gives a general depiction of what the stamp elements look like.

§ 13.3.5 Advanced Options Section

The Advanced Options section of the IntelliPDF BATES dialog box has six tabs for specifying the creation method (Creation), the number of copies (Copies), whether or not to create bookmarks (Bookmarks), whether to use batch mode, which allows the stamp to be applied serially to a group of PDF documents (Batch Mode), whether to scale or shift the content so that it is not covered by the stamp (Scale), and a file lookup window to browse for saved sets of preferences (Preferences). The Creation tab lets you choose between applying the stamp to the original document or creating a copy of the original document and stamping the copy. The default setting calls for the stamp to be applied to a copy; a good idea, because once the file has been saved the stamp cannot be removed. The Copies tab lets you decide how many copies of the stamped document to generate. The copy has the name of the original with "_Bates" appended at the end. If the Bookmark option is checked, the plug-in generates a bookmark for each Bates stamp. This helps you to navigate within the stamped pages. Bates stamp bookmarks appear under the section of the bookmarks area. The Scale tab allows you to scale a page content while stamping to prevent stamps from overriding the content of the source document. Use the Move Content To option to adjust the position of the scaled page content. Finally, the Preferences tab can be used to set up a default path for storing your stamp profiles (presets).

§ 13.3.6 Full Preview Section and Action Buttons

The Full Preview section of the IntelliPDF Bates dialog box displays the current page of the open PDF document, showing the placement of the stamp or stamps that have been set up. The action buttons at the bottom right of the dialog box are to Load a preset stamp profile, Save the current profile as a preset, Stamp to apply the current stamp or stamps to the open document, and Cancel (quit without saving or stamping).

§ 13.4 Redacting Information

When you share documents with others electronically, the need to redact sensitive information arises eventually. Whether you are sending PDFs to opposing counsel or the court, you will some day need to redact privileged or confidential information. Courts are adopting policies that require counsel to redact personal and sensitive information from documents filed with the court that will be open to public access. Redax 3.5, also from Appligent, is a plug-in for Acrobat that is designed to completely remove text and scanned images from PDF files. You can use Redax to edit PDF files that need sensitive or privileged information removed before they are made public or shared with opposing counsel. To use Redax with image-on-text files, you simply open a document in Acrobat, then with the click of a menu command Redax searches the document, tags the words specified in a selected text file, and overlays them with the corresponding exemption codes (text, white space, or black space). Each tagged selection can be resized, moved, or deleted. Click another command and a new document is created, and the redacted text is replaced with the exemption codes and deleted. Save the new, redacted document, and it's ready for public viewing or sharing with opposing counsel. To create a privilege log, Redax automatically generates a text file of the final redactions that can be imported into a spreadsheet for printing or for future analysis and reference.

Redax can also be used on image-only files, but with certain limitations. First, because there is no text in image-only files, Redax cannot search and tag specific terms to be redacted. Likewise, Redax cannot generate a text file for use as a privilege log. When working with image-only files, Redax replaces all pixels in the selected area with black pixels. Because pixels are replaced, rather than overlaid, the redacted information cannot be extracted from the final document.

Display Mode | **14**

Beginning with Version 6.0, Acrobat contains a great feature called Full Screen view. Think of Full Screen view as display mode. In display mode, the toolbars, menus, and navigation panes disappear, and the current page of the open PDF file fills the screen. Because computer displays do not have the same height-to-width ratio as most PDF files (typically based on standard paper sizes), the image has a border that fills the screen.

Documents displayed in portrait orientation show more border than documents displayed in landscape orientation. The color of the border can be set in the Preferences dialog box, in the Full Screen section (Background Color).

You can use this feature for presentations in the office, in court, or anywhere else. Display mode can be used to present exhibits at trial, much like specialized trial-presentation applications. There are limits to display mode, but they can be overcome quickly if you are willing to drop back to the standard view for highlighting and zooming in on portions of a page. The shift from display mode to normal and back again can be done in the blink of an eye using the keyboard commands. The process of shifting between Full Screen view and one of the standard page views may seem clunky at first but with use will become smooth and second nature.

Before we go into the details, you might be wondering why you would want to use Acrobat for presentations, rather than Microsoft PowerPoint. The short answer is that if you prepare your presentation in PowerPoint and then print (or publish) it to PDF, anyone with Acrobat Reader can view it. Your audience does not need to have PowerPoint or use the same operating system as you. Your presentation is relatively secure in that you have not sent the viewer the native application file (in PowerPoint format). If your presentation includes full images of pages of original documents, then inserting those full pages into an Acrobat document works much better than trying to show a full 8$\frac{1}{2}$-by-11 page in PowerPoint. Keep in mind that PowerPoint is presentation software, while Acrobat is digital document software. If you need to give a presentation, then PowerPoint might be the better tool. On the other hand, if you need to display and work with digital documents, then Acrobat is the better choice. If you need to give a presentation that includes digital documents, prepare the slides using PowerPoint, print the slide show to PDF, and then insert documents at the desired locations.

Coupling Acrobat's display mode with Adobe Photoshop (or even the consumer-grade Photoshop Elements) creates a beefed-up tool. Using Photoshop Elements you can create a PDF slide show from a mixed collection of PDF image-only or image-on-text documents and photographs. This can be especially useful when combining mixed files into a single PDF for use as a trial exhibit notebook. With Photoshop Elements you can take that huge collection of digital photograph files (JPEG, TIFF, PSD, and so on) that your client, investigator, or expert witness gave you and convert them to a single multipage PDF document. That document can then be enhanced with bookmarks, links, comments, and Bates numbers.

§ 14.1 Using Full Screen View

If you think that Full Screen view, or display mode, would be accessed through the View menu, you're thinking the right way, but you reached the wrong conclusion. Full Screen view is accessed through the Window menu.

> Menu (Full Screen View): **Window** > **Full Screen View**
> Keystroke (Full Screen View): **Ctrl+L**
> or
> Keystroke (Full Screen View): **Alt+W-F**

Once in display mode you navigate by using the keyboard or mouse. To advance one page, use the Page Down key, Down Arrow key, Right Arrow key, or left-click.

To go back one page, use the Page Up key, the Up Arrow key, the Left Arrow key, or right-click.

To advance to a specific page while in Full Screen view:

> Keystroke (Go To Page): **Shift+Ctrl+N**

The **Go To Page** dialog box appears; simply key in the desired page number and press **Enter** or click **OK**. (See Figures 14.1 and 14.2)

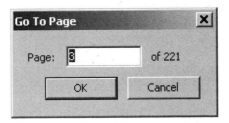

Figure 14.1

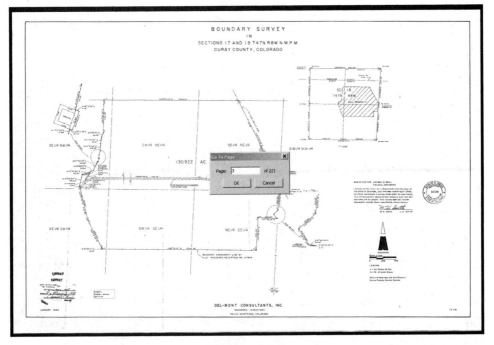

Figure 14.2

Using the Go To Page *n* function allows you to jump from one exhibit (image) to another in a nonlinear manner so long as you have a list of the page numbers on which each exhibit (image) begins. You jump to the first page of the exhibit then use the Page Down, Arrow Down, Right Arrow keys or left click to advance one page at a time.

To leave Full Screen view (display mode) and return to the normal view, simply press the **Esc** (Escape) key:

Keystroke (Return to Normal View): **Esc**

§ 14.2 PDF Exhibit Notebook

Using Acrobat to create a trial exhibit notebook and then using Full Screen view to display those exhibits at trial is easy and very effective. Here are the basic instructions (you might find a quicker and better way to do this):

First, assuming that all of your exhibits exist as PDF files, mark each for use at trial. Most courts have rules (or at least preferences) for how exhibits are marked. For example, all plaintiff's exhibits are numbered while the defendant's exhibits are lettered.

Next, create an exhibit log (you should probably do this for the other side's exhibits as well). The log can be as simple as the following table:

Exhibit	Page #	Description	Stipulated (Y/N)	Offered (Y/N)	Admitted (Y/N)

Table 14.1

Next, use a word processing application to create a one-page document that says something like:

Defendant's Trial Exhibits

Gotham Superior Court

Case Number 2004CV500

Print this page to PDF and use it as the first page of your exhibit notebook. It also serves as a place to park your presentation so that the judge and jury aren't left to stare at an exhibit (unless you want them to). See Figure 14.3.

Once you have created your cover page and have your exhibits marked for identification, combine all the pages into a single PDF file (name it something like AllTrialExhibits.pdf). Start with the cover page and insert the exhibits one at a time. As you insert exhibits, do two things: (1) put the beginning page number in the log on the row for that exhibit, and (2) create a bookmark at the beginning of each exhibit (use names like "1 Smith-Jones Contract" and "2 Smith to Jones Deed"). The page number on the exhibit log and bookmarks assumes that you have exhibits of more than one page. If all your exhibits are only one page, then you could probably get by with renumbering the pages (using virtual page numbering; see Chapter 6). You can then jump to any point in the document by page number. During trial you can nav-

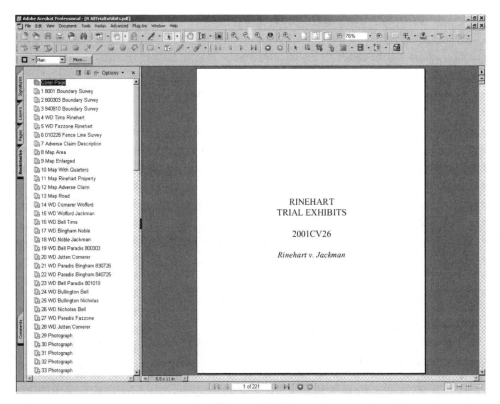

Figure 14.3

igate between exhibits in normal view using the Bookmarks pane or by using the Go To Page function (using the exhibit log to determine the first page of the desired exhibit). As a bonus, use the log to keep track of what exhibits were admitted by stipulation, offered and admitted, or offered and denied. The judge, courtroom clerk, and opposing counsel will appreciate receiving copies of the exhibit logs. If you copy all your exhibits to CD-ROM to give copies to the court and opposing counsel, they can use the log to go to a specific page in the exhibit notebook.

To use the Acrobat exhibit notebook during trial, display the cover page and bookmarks. When you want a witness to talk about a particular exhibit, click on the bookmark for that exhibit, lay an appropriate foundation, move to admit, and then use the exhibit. For example:

> **Counsel:** I call your attention to the screen where I am displaying what has been marked for identification as Exhibit 16; are you familiar with subject of the photograph?
>
> **Witness:** Yes.
>
> **Counsel:** Explain the basis of your familiarity with the subject of the photograph.

Witness: It's a picture that I took of the scene of the accident.

Counsel: Is the photograph a good, fair, accurate, or true representation of the accident scene?

Witness: Yes.

Counsel: Your Honor, I move for the admission of Exhibit 16.

If you "park" the display on the cover page in Full Screen view, press **Ctrl+Shift+N,** enter the beginning page number of the desired exhibit, and then press **Enter** or click **OK.**

If you display the exhibit in Full Screen view (**Ctrl+L**), you can still zoom in or out without returning to normal view. However, zooming (magnifying) in display mode only works on the center of the current document; if you need to zoom in on something beyond the center (say information in the upper right-hand corner), you'll need to go back to the normal view and use the dynamic zoom tool.

To zoom in (magnify) while in display mode:

Menu: None

Keystroke (Zoom In Full Screen View): **Ctrl+M**, then select or type the desired magnification

Experiment in your office with ways to organize and display exhibits using Acrobat. As you develop a system that you are comfortable with, practice it. Practice in your office using Acrobat to review exhibits before depositions or trial. Practice using Acrobat to present exhibits during depositions. In a short time you will become comfortable using Acrobat to organize and present exhibits. When that happens, there will be no more shuffling of paper in the courtroom.

§ 14.3 Full Screen View Preferences

You can set default preferences for how Full Screen view looks and acts. To access the Preferences dialog box:

Menu (Full Screen Preferences): **Edit** > **Preferences**
Keystroke (Full Screen Preferences): **Ctrl+K**

When the **Preferences** dialog box appears, select **Full Screen** in the window on the left (Figure 14.4).

The dialog box now has two parts: Full Screen Navigation and Full Screen Appearance. In the Navigation section, you can set Acrobat to advance one page at a time, at a set interval, whenever documents are displayed in Full

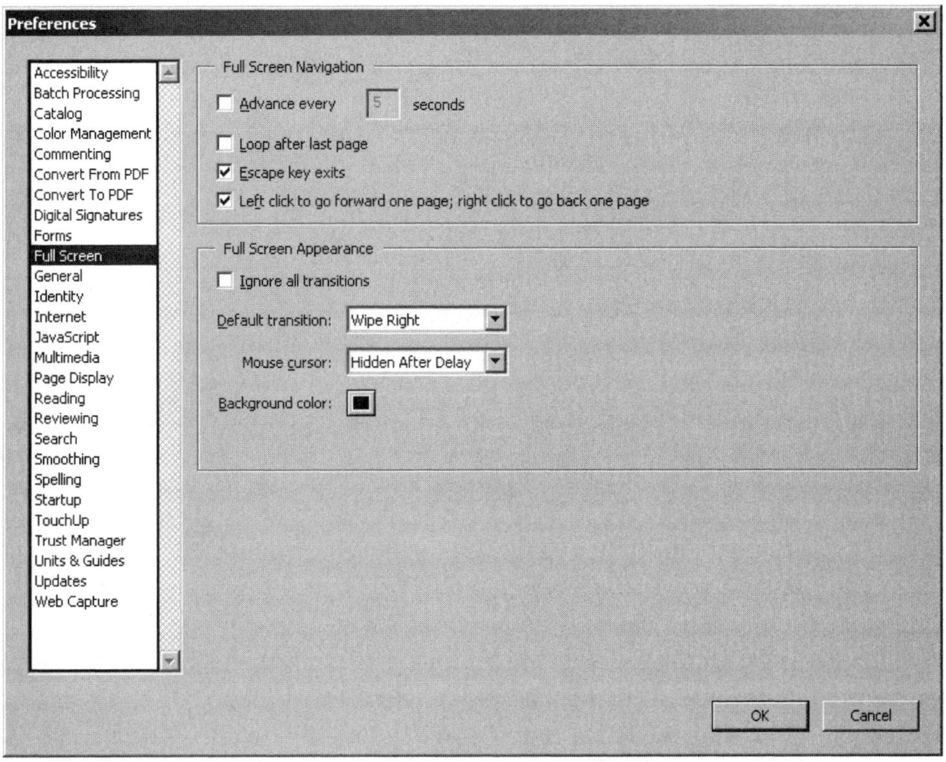

Figure 14.4

Screen view. Leaving the **Advance every __ seconds** box unchecked requires you to manually advance the pages. If you want Acrobat to continually advance through the pages, check the **Loop after last page** box. When the **Escape key exits** box is unchecked, the only way to exit Full Screen view is to close the document with the keyboard command **Ctrl+F4.** Acrobat 7.0 adds another option in the Full Screen Navigation section. You can now check a box to **Show Navigation Bar,** which will put three icons in the lower left portion of the full screen display that represent Forward One Page, Back One Page, and Escape. Check the **Left click to go forward one page; right click to go back one page** box to make left-clicks advance one page and right-clicks go back one page.

The bottom section of the Full Screen Preferences dialog box controls the default appearance whenever documents are displayed in Full Screen view. You can select from a number of transition types (how one page replaces another); or whether the pointer (**Mouse cursor**) is always hidden, always visible, or hidden after a delay. Finally, you can set the **Background color** (border color) to any shade that your computer can display (some computers can display more colors than others).

E-briefs 15

This chapter brings together some of the material from other chapters in a practical explanation of how to use Acrobat to create electronic briefs. While the e-brief is used as the exemplar here, do not limit your thinking to just briefs. Consider complex communications to clients with multiple enclosures, or detailed in-house research memos.

§ 15.1 Why Acrobat for E-briefs?

Most appellate court rules do not presently provide for the filing of electronic briefs. However, many courts have expressed an interest in receiving electronic briefs and are in the process of developing internal and public rules. This chapter describes in detail how to create complex digital or electronic documents.

Many courts and government agencies have adopted PDF as the standard file format. Accordingly, the process detailed here relies on Acrobat for assembling the electronic brief. Acrobat also provides a means to convert paper documents to electronic copies that can be attached or linked to the brief. It would be hard to imagine a law firm today not using a computer and word processing application to generate a brief for filing with the court. Because almost all documents generated in the typical law firm are created electronically, the process described here begins at the point when the brief has been completed and would be printed on paper and signed.

§ 15.2 Printing a Markup Copy

Before printing the final word processing file to PDF, print it on paper. The responsible lawyer should review the paper version and mark all references that are linked to source materials (cases, statutes, transcripts, the record on appeal, and so on). Consider also whether the links should appear in a color other than black. Indicating links by way of a different font color helps the reader know where links exist. The tasks of creating the links, changing the color of the text, and assembling the electronic brief can all be delegated to a staff person who works from the printed version with highlighted references.

§ 15.3 Printing to PDF

To print the final brief word processing file to PDF, use a print command within the native application that allows for printer selection (WordPerfect: **File** > **Print,** or **Ctrl+P,** or **F5;** Word: **File** > **Print**, or **Ctrl+P**), and then choose a printer driver that prints to PDF (see also Section 4.1). When Acrobat 6.0 or 7.0 have been installed on a computer, the installation routine adds a new virtual printer, Adobe PDF (Acrobat 4.0 and 5.0 installed two virtual printers to the system, Acrobat PDFWriter and Acrobat Distiller). With these virtual printers, any file on the computer that can be printed to a hardware printer can be printed to PDF. Certain image-file types, such as JPEG, TIFF, and BMP, can be printed to PDF by dragging and dropping the file icon (for example, from Windows Explorer) onto the empty Acrobat document window.

§ 15.4 Scanning to PDF

To use Acrobat to create a PDF document by scanning (see also Section 4.2), from the **File** menu select **Create PDF** > **From Scanner,** or use keystrokes (**Alt+F-F-N** Version 6.0; **Alt+F-F-S** Version 7.0). At this point in the process, check the settings for paper size, resolution, and whether the documents will pass through a feeder. Once the document has finished scanning, you have the option to add more pages to the scanner and pages to the PDF document being created, or to save what you have to a file. When **Done** has been selected, the scanned image appears in the document window. To save the document image, from the **File** menu select **Save** or press **Ctrl+S** on the keyboard, and a dialog box opens that allows you to select an appropriate folder and assign a file name.

Scan documents at a resolution of 300 dots per inch (dpi). That resolution produces near-photocopy quality when printed. In order to minimize the size of scanned image files, select scanner output settings for **black and white** (sometimes listed as **text** or **line drawing**). Select color or gray scale output settings only when necessary (these settings produce substantially larger files). If the documents to be scanned contain drawings, handwritten notes, or the like (content not susceptible to OCR), prepare a document summary (see Figure 15.1):

Menu (Create Document Summary): **File** > **Document Properties** > **Summary,** then enter a description

Keystroke (Create Document Summary): **Alt+F-D,** then enter a description

or

Keystroke (Create Document Summary): **Crtl+D,** then enter a description

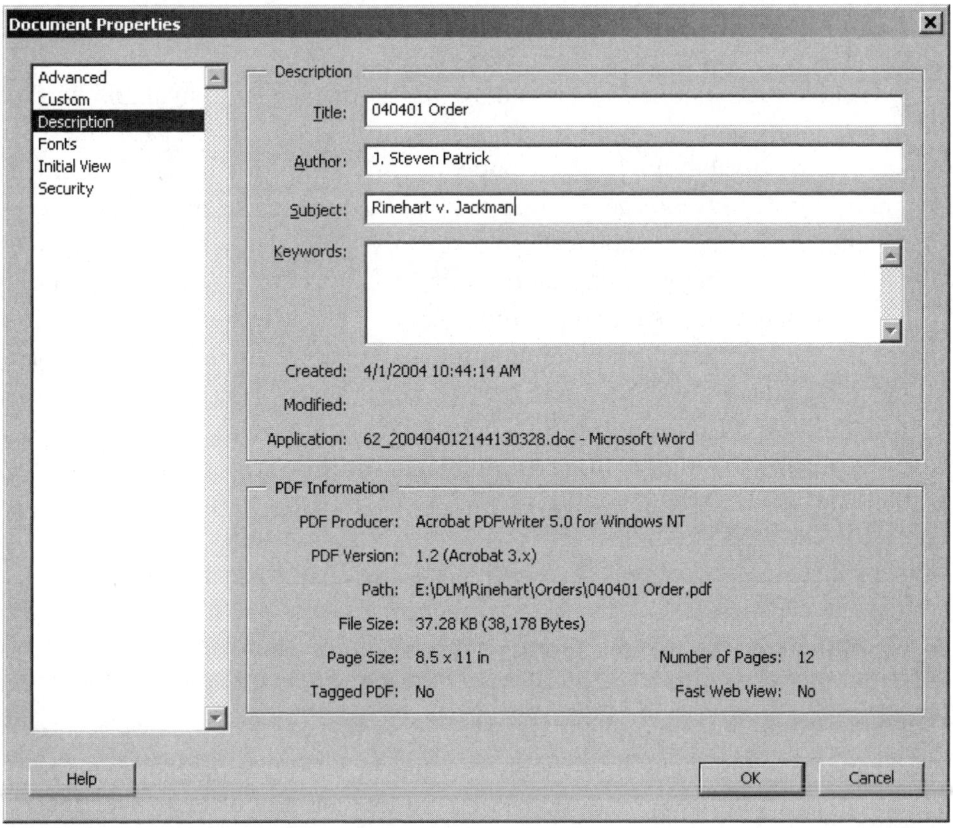

Figure 15.1

The **Document Properties** dialog box opens. Select **Description** from the window on the left. The information included in the document summary is included in any index generated and provides a means to locate the document using the Acrobat or Windows Explorer search function.

§ 15.5 Creating and Organizing the Source Materials

When possible, source materials (such as cases, statutes, and trial transcripts) should be printed to PDF from an existing digital source. For example, case law retrieved from an online source or CD-ROM can be printed directly to PDF. Use short logical names for these materials, such as a short form of their citation (such as "Whinnery 895P2d537"). Observance of this naming convention results in the cases arranging themselves in alphabetical order, making them easier to locate when building the links. Avoid using periods, commas, and other punctuation marks when naming these files. Whenever possible, obtain digital copies of transcripts. Using a transcript management application such as RealLegal Binder, Summation, LiveNote, or TextMap, print the transcript to PDF. Alternatively, open the transcript file in a word processing application, adjust the formatting as necessary (often a frustrating process), and then print the file to PDF.

Some source materials to be linked to the brief are not available in digital format. For example, copies of contracts, answers to interrogatories, or affidavits may only be available in paper form. These documents should be scanned and, if they are good copies or originals contain mostly text, then these images should be converted to text by OCR. By performing OCR on these documents they become searchable, and links can be made to pinpoint locations. OCR can be performed from within Acrobat by selecting Paper Capture from the Document menu (**Document** > **Paper Capture** > **Start Capture**, or by using keystrokes: **Alt+D-U-S**). Some third-party OCR applications convert PDF image files, retaining an exact copy of the original while creating a text file behind the image. Keep in mind that OCR does not produce perfect results; the primary purpose is to provide a text background that can be searched for quick reference.

§ 15.6 Planning and Organization

Decide whether the reference materials will be attached to the original document (by inserting pages), or maintained as separate document files. Short works, such as motions, lend themselves to inclusion of all reference materials; longer, more complex documents, such as appellate briefs, should link to external documents. No precise guideline can be stated for when to do one or the other, nor have the courts promulgated rules addressing this issue. The detailed procedures described below address both all-in-one documents (simple electronic briefs) and documents with links to external reference materials (complex electronic briefs).

If producing a complex electronic brief, the linking process must be performed on the local hard disk drive. In other words, the final PDF version of the brief and all source materials must exist on the local C drive. This step must be observed—building the complex electronic brief on a network drive results in nonfunctional links when the final product is transferred to CD.

§ 15.6.1 Organization of Complex Electronic Briefs

To begin this process, create a folder for the project, such as CD Smith Brief (using this convention, rather than Smith Brief CD, places all the CD projects in the same area of the hard disk drive when viewed through Windows Explorer). Within the project folder, create subfolders for briefs and source materials, for example:

> Briefs (C:\CD Smith Brief\Brief)
>> Authorities (C:\CD Smith Brief\Authorities)
>>> Cases (C:\CD Smith Brief\Authorities\Cases)
>>> Statutes (C:\CD Smith Brief\Authorities\Statutes)
>>> Regulations (C:\CD Smith Brief\Authorities\Regulations)
>>> CourtRules (C:\CD Smith Brief\Authorities\CourtRules)
> Transcripts (C:\ CD Smith Brief\Transcripts)
> Record (C:\ CD Smith Brief\Record)

A set of empty folders can be created and saved for repeated use. This provides a standard taxonomy for all electronic brief disks generated in the future (Figure 15.2).

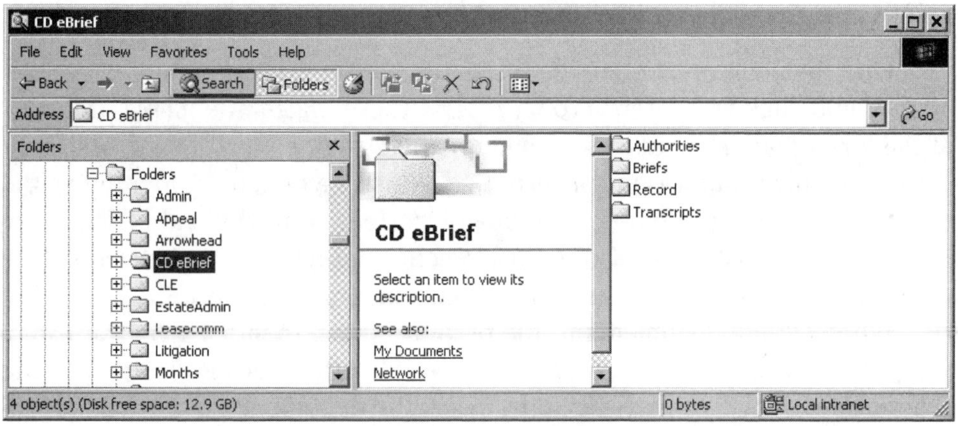

Figure 15.2

A staff person can retrieve cases and statutes from online or CD-ROM sources, print them to PDF, and save them to the appropriate folders. Scan the record to PDF (this way the images of the record on the final CD have the numbering supplied by the trial court appellate clerk). After scanning the record, run the file through an OCR application such as OmniPagePro or the Capture feature in Acrobat.

> Menu (Paper Capture): **Document** > **Paper Capture** > **Start Capture**
> Keystroke (Paper Capture): **Alt+D-U-S**

If the trial court provides an electronic record, then this step is not necessary.

§ 15.6.2 Organization of Simple Electronic Briefs

The simple electronic brief process may be done at any work station with Adobe Acrobat. Because the brief file and source files are combined into a single PDF document, the final product may exist on a network drive and need not be copied to the local drive. The CD may be recorded from a network source but may work better when the source file exists on the local hard disk drive of the CD-R machine.

When the brief has reached its final form (ready to be printed, and the linked references are color-changed if desired), print it to PDF. Using Acrobat, open the document and bookmark the major divisions (including the first page) by going to the desired location and pressing **Ctrl-B.** After creating the bookmarks, go to the end of the document (**Ctrl+Shift+Page Down** or **Ctrl+End**), and insert the first item to be linked. To insert this document:

> 6.0 Menu (Insert Pages): **Document** > **Pages** > **Insert**
> 7.0 Menu (Insert Pages): **Document** > **Insert Pages**
> Keystroke (Insert Pages): **Ctrl+Shift+I**

Find the file representing the pages to be inserted, highlight and double-click it, and click **OK**. After Acrobat inserts these pages, the display remains at the former last page of the document; advance one page (to the first page of the document that was just inserted), and insert a bookmark identifying the document. After these pages have been inserted, go to the end of the document (now the last page of the most recently inserted file), and repeat the process until all source materials have been incorporated into the brief.

When adding documents to the original, group them by type (for example, put all the cases in first, then the transcripts, then the affidavits, then the other exhibits); within each grouping insert the documents in the order of appearance in the pleading. Think of this as taking photocopies of the cases cited and grouping them together in the order of appearance, then taking a group of transcripts, putting them in order, and attaching them to the growing document. Creating the links to documents that have been inserted into the original document is discussed later.

§ 15.7 Creating the Links

Links are the heart and soul of electronic briefs. Links make electronic briefs interactive and truly powerful. When a citation to a case, statute, or other authority appears in your brief, it can be linked to the cited material so that with a click of the mouse the reader sees the authority you have cited. While the next section describes the process for creating links, you may wish to review Section 6.2 for a more detailed discussion on creating links.

§ 15.7.1 The Mechanics

Using Acrobat, the responsible lawyer or a staff person opens the brief and begins building the links. Find the first reference in the brief to be linked to a source. Click on the **Link** tool; it looks like the links of chain and appears only on the Advanced Editing toolbar (see also Section 6.2).

To display the Advanced Editing toolbar, from the **View** menu select **Toolbars** > **Advanced Editing.** Next drag a box around the citation (full case name, reference to record, reference to exhibit, and so on), choose **Open a page in this document**, Version 6.0; choose **Go to page view** in Version 7.0, or **Open a file,** then set the link destination. The Create Link dialog box in Version 7.0 allows you to set the appearance of the link. Assuming that you select Invisible Rectangle, then, after the link has been created and with the Link Tool active, right-click on the link and select **Make Current Properties Default.** There are a few more steps for those using Version 6.0. After completing the first link, with the Link tool still active, right-click on the newly created link and select **Properties.** In the Properties window select **Invisible Rectangle** from the **Link Type** drop-down menu and select **Close.** Right-click again on the newly created link and select **Use Current Appearance as New Default.** Continue through the brief, setting links. Selecting **Open a file** in the **Create Link** window displays a dialog box permitting location and selection of the destination file. To make the link go to a specific page in the destination file, after completing the link and with the Link tool still active, double-click on the link; from the **Actions** tab, select **Go to a page in another document** from the drop-down list, click **Add** and browse to locate the destination file, select the destination file, specify the page number the link should open to, and select **Close.**

In the simple electronic brief, where all source materials are inserted into the original document, the linking process is easier. Go to the first item to be linked, select the **Link** tool, drag a box around the citation or reference, and choose **Open a page in this document**, Version 6.0; choose **Go to page view** in Version 7.0. Insert the page number for the link destination and click **OK.** Once the link has been established, the dialog box closes. After completing the first link and with the Link tool still active, right-click on the newly created link and select **Properties.** In the Properties window select **Invisible Rectangle** from the **Link Type** drop-down menu and select **Close.** Right-click again on the newly created link and select **Use Current Appearance as New Default.** Continue working through the document building links. After all links have been made, a test CD should be given to another staff person, so he or she can walk through the brief, confirming that all links work properly.

§ 15.7.2 Stylistic Considerations

Each brief should include a table of contents with links to the various sections. The table of authorities should link to the first page of source materials. Within the brief, specific citations should be pinpointed whenever appropriate.

§ 15.8 Copying the Finished Product to CD

Creating a CD containing one or more briefs and cited materials requires that the linking process be performed on the local hard disk drive. In other words, the final PDF version of the brief and all source materials must exist on the local C drive (not a network drive). This step must be observed—building the complex electronic brief on a network drive results in nonfunctional links when the final product is transferred to CD. If the folder structure described in Section 15.6.1 has been followed, then the contents page, the "About this CD" file, the files and folders created by cataloging or indexing the materials, and the auto-run feature are in the root folder C:\CD Smith Brief (see Figure 15.3).

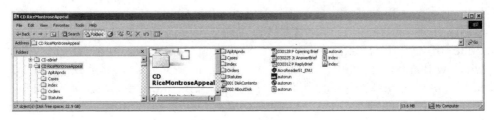

Figure 15.3

§ 15.8.1 Creating and Including a Contents Page

A contents page may be included as a convenience to the court and to others who read the briefs. The contents page is a simple document, prepared with a word processing application and then printed to PDF, listing the primary objects on the disk; each item in the list is linked to the appropriate destination. A sample contents page can be found at the end of this chapter.

The contents page, if included, is opened by the auto-run application. In this way, a user places the CD-ROM in a drive and the contents page automatically opens. Then from the contents page the reader can navigate to the desired brief or record volume by clicking on links.

§ 15.8.2 Creating and Including an "About this CD" File

Include an "About this CD" file on the CD-ROM to aid users. A sample file appears at the end of the chapter. This page provides a place where the user can find a description of the organization and structure of the CD. It also provides a place to describe any errata or special features of the briefs and record compiled on the CD.

§ 15.8.3 Indexing the CD Contents

You can use the Acrobat Catalog feature (Figure 15.4) to create a full-text index of PDF documents or document collections. Creating a full-text index can speed up the search process. This can be helpful if large PDF document collections of appellate documents need to be searched repeatedly. Note that information contained in comments and document descriptions related to image-only PDF documents are included in the index and found using the Search function. To create an index:

> Menu (Catalog): **Advanced** > **Catalog**, then select **New Index**
> Keystroke (Catalog): **Alt+A-T**, then select **New Index**

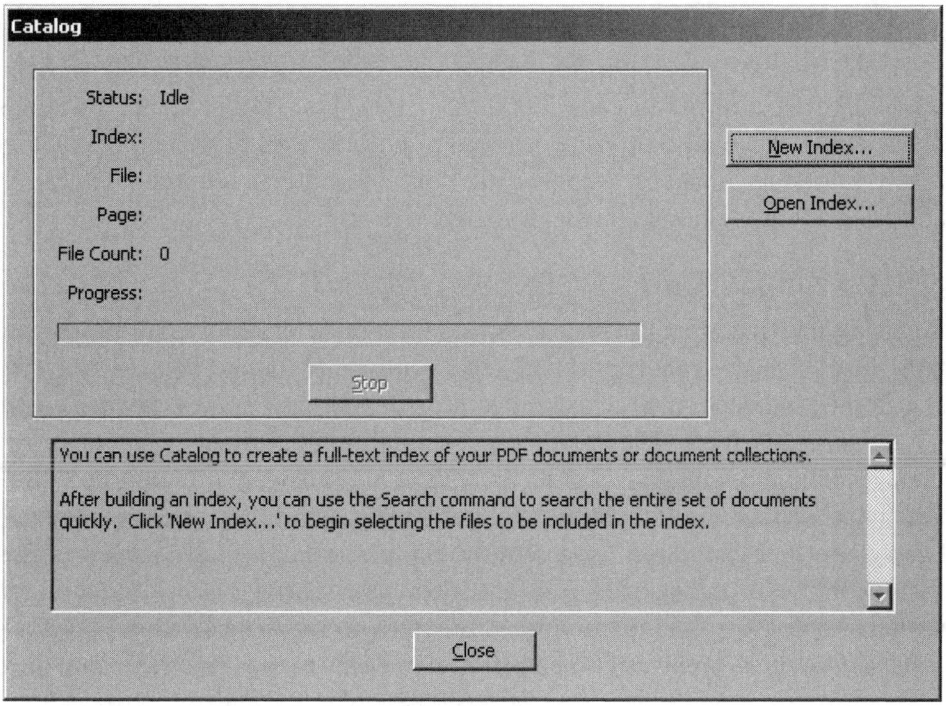

Catalog

Status: Idle
Index:
File:
Page:
File Count: 0
Progress:

[New Index...]
[Open Index...]

[Stop]

You can use Catalog to create a full-text index of your PDF documents or document collections.

After building an index, you can use the Search command to search the entire set of documents quickly. Click 'New Index...' to begin selecting the files to be included in the index.

[Close]

Figure 15.4

The **Catalog** dialog box opens. Select **New Index,** type a name for the index, select the folders (directories) that contain the PDF documents to be included in the index (you can also select subdirectories to be excluded), and click **Build.** When you build a new index, the results are a new .pdx file and a new folder (named Index) that contains one or more .idx files. The .pdx file, which is small, makes the information in the .idx files available to the search function. The .idx files contain the index entries that a user finds in the index, so their file sizes—individually or collectively—can be large. All of these files must be available to users who want to search the index.

§ 15.8.4 Adding an Auto-run Feature

The auto-run feature does what the name implies; when a CD-ROM is inserted into the computer, it causes an application (Reader or Acrobat) to open a specified file. For e-briefs you need only a rudimentary auto-run application to instruct the computer to open a specific file, typically the contents page file described above in Section 15.8.1. To find an application that creates the auto-run feature, Google "autorun" and browse through the results until you find what you need.

§ 15.9 Service and Filing

At present, few appellate courts have developed rules for service and filing of electronic briefs. If your court has established rules, by all means follow them; otherwise, two alternatives are described below. While either meets the needs of the court, it would be most desirable to end up with all briefs, cases, and record materials linked on a single disk. Both alternatives require cooperation and coordination among counsel for the parties.

§ 15.9.1 Alternative 1

In this alternative, the appellant files the opening brief on disk. The disk contains the brief, the record, and all legal authorities cited. The brief is constructed with links to the record and authorities. Next, the appellee files an answer brief on CD-ROM. The appellee's disk contains a copy of everything from the appellant's opening-brief disk, as well as the answer brief and any additional authorities cited. If contents pages were used, a new one is generated. Finally, the appellant files and serves the reply brief. This disk contains everything from the opening-brief disk and the answer-brief disk along with the reply brief and any additional authorities cited. Again, if contents pages are used, a new one is created with links to the primary materials on the final disk.

§ 15.9.2 Alternative 2

In this alternative a single disk, containing all briefs, the record, and legal authorities, is filed at some point after all the paper filings have been submitted to the court. This alternative has the hallmark of simplicity, eliminates the task of creating electronic versions of briefs contemporaneously with the paper versions, and allows either or both parties to participate in creating the final product.

Sample Contents Page

CD CONTENTS

[Click Here for Information about this CD]

Appellant's Opening Brief

Appellee's Joint Answer Brief

Appellant's Reply Brief

Record

> Volume I
>
> Volume II
>
> Volume III
>
> Volume IV
>
> Volume V
>
> Volume VI
>
> Volume VII

Cases

Statutes

Court Rules

Miscellaneous

Sample "About this CD" File

ABOUT THIS CD

<u>Rationale</u>. This CD was prepared by _____, as a convenience to the court and counsel. If your computer has a CD-ROM drive and Adobe Acrobat or Acrobat Reader, you need only insert the CD; it should auto-run and open to a CD Contents page. If it does not auto-run, use Windows Explorer, Acrobat, or the Reader program to open the file "001 Contents."

<u>Errata</u>. While preparing the digital versions of these briefs we noticed several typographical errors in _____. We did not correct the errors but did make the links to incorrectly cited cases and statutes go to the appropriate documents.

<u>File Format</u>. All files on this CD are in Adobe Portable Document Format (PDF). There are image-only PDFs and image-on-text files. Image-only PDFs are just that; images only, just digital photocopies of paper documents. Image-on-text files have an exact image of the hard copy with text behind the image. Image-on-text files are created by printing to PDF or by running a PDF image-only file through an optical character recognition (OCR) application. On this CD, the first nine pages of Appellant's opening brief were scanned and then OCR'd; the remainder of the opening brief was obtained from Appellant's counsel in PDF format. The Appellant's Appendix was scanned; no OCR was performed on the Appendix; thus, the Appendix consists of PDF image-only files. The Appellant's reply brief was scanned and OCR'd. The Appellee's answer brief was printed to PDF, as were all of the cases and selected statutes.

<u>Links</u>. The Table of Contents in each brief has been linked to the appropriate section in the body of the brief. Additionally, references to the record and citations to case law have been linked to their respective sources. Note: the links are not color coded. Move the pointer over a citation to the record or case law, when the "hand" changes to a hand with a "pointing finger," click and referenced material is displayed. To return to the main document use the Return to Previous View button. If you drill down very far into the documents, it may be easiest simply to reopen the main contents file, rather than clicking the Return to Previous View button numerous times.

<u>File Structure</u>. The CD has been set to auto-run and open to the CD Contents page. All of the cases cited by the parties are collected in a folder named Cases. There are no links from the CD Contents page to the individual cases (there are links from the Table of Authorities to each case). Each volume of the Appellant's Appendix has been included in a folder named ApltApndx. Statutes cited by Appellee have been reproduced and linked. Court rules cited by the parties have not been reproduced and linked.

Acrobat in the Paperless Office 16

This chapter brings together material from other parts of the book in a practical explanation of how to use Acrobat as the foundation for a paperless office. Because Acrobat allows us to handle digital documents in ways similar to how we work with paper documents, it can provide the foundation for a paperless office.

§ 16.1 Why Go Paperless with Acrobat?

Consider for a moment what it would be like to be able to find documents at your desk without rummaging through file cabinets or boxes. Think of all the paper you put in files because someday you might need it, only to never see it again. Consider the unpleasant process of closing those files and moving them to storage. Recall the times you've gone to storage to retrieve a single piece of paper. Now, consider keeping all those documents in electronic format, readily available if needed, and then closing files by dragging them from an active work directory to an archive directory.

Paper takes up space, weighs a lot, becomes misplaced or even lost, and is just plain cumbersome to work with. Your client brings you three banker boxes of documents. You spend hours sifting and organizing the documents into folders, which are in turn organized in various redwells. You spend hours rummaging through the folders and redwells knowing that *one* document can be found in there—somewhere. On the day of trial you pull out the trust dolly and load up your redwells and boxes and head to the courthouse. The redwells are splitting at the seams; they begin to fray and tear. Then opposing counsel makes mention of that *one* special document. Your fingers race through the pages, folders, and redwells. There is an easier way: go paperless; go digital; go PDF; go Acrobat.

Acrobat provides good image acquisition capabilities (the ability to perform OCR on the images while retaining an exact image of the scanned pages) and easy sharing with other users. Federal and state courts that have activated systems for the electronic filing of documents have settled on PDF as the standard. If the courts are using PDF, then it should be a good standard for use in the office.

In addition to using Acrobat for creating PDF files by acquiring images with a scanner or printing image-on-text PDF files from native applications, you can use Acrobat to make the PDF files truly useful. For example, you can add bookmarks and sticky notes to image-only files. If the files have a text background, you can highlight (pick your color–any color), underline, and strike through. PDF files with background text can be searched; image-only files cannot be searched but information contained in the Document Summary or in attached notes is included in indexes of document collections.

§ 16.2 Law Office Information Systems

Lawyers and law firms process information. We receive information from clients and other sources, we add information gained from research and experience, and we deliver information. The information that lawyers deliver takes many forms. It may be a pleading, an oral presentation to a court, an opinion letter, or an agreement; but in the end, lawyers process and deliver information.

Most of the information that comes into the law office arrives in the form of documents. For that matter, most of the information output from law offices—work product—goes out as some form of document. Taking a very simple and abstract view of the typical law office, there are three primary systems involved in processing documents:

- ◆ A document generation system
- ◆ A document copying or replication system
- ◆ A document retention or filing system

The document generation system includes more than computers and printers; it includes fax machines, couriers, and the daily mail. The outside sources generate as many documents as the internal systems—documents that contain information that lawyers need to analyze, store, and retrieve. When documents come into the law office, the information system looks something like Figure 16.1.

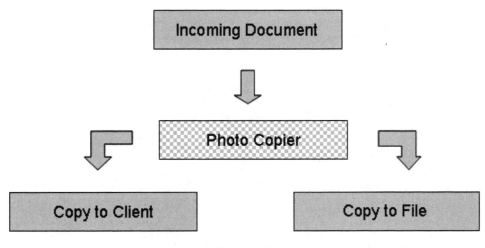

Figure 16.1

When the law firm generates a document for delivery to a third party, the information system looks like Figure 16.2.

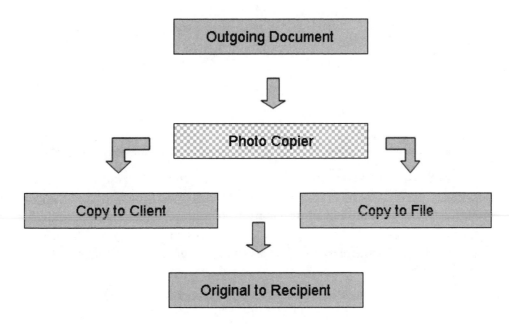

Figure 16.2

In addition to the basic incoming and outgoing document scenarios, we should take a look at the special case of litigation documents. When a collection of documents comes in during litigation, whether from the client or an opposing party, they are typically preserved as a clean set, which is then photocopied and Bates numbered. The Bates numbered set is then copied to create a file set, a working set, and sets for distribution to other parties. When dealing with litigation documents, the typical law office information system looks something like this Figure 16.3.

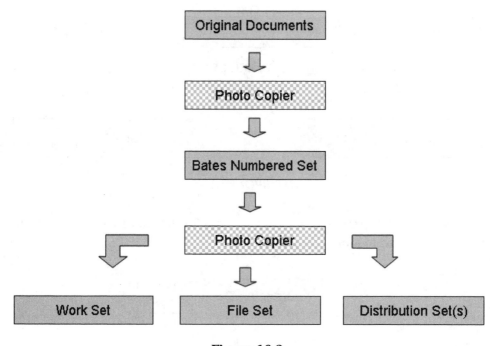

Figure 16.3

§ 16.3 Basic Document Management

In the preceding illustrations, documents (whether incoming or outgoing) pass through the copying or replication system. In the typical office, a photocopier acts as the copying or replication system. In the paperless office, a scanner replaces the photocopier. Incoming documents pass through the scanner, rather than a photocopier, producing digital copies that are stored electronically. Outgoing documents, rather than being scanned or photocopied, are retained in their original digital format and printed (converted) to the same format as scanned documents. Digital copies can be replicated at will, quickly and easily.

When documents come into the paperless law office, the information processing system changes only slightly from the photocopier paper-based system. It looks like Figure 16.4.

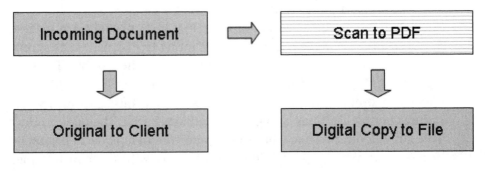

Figure 16.4

At the other end of the process, when the law firm generates outgoing documents, the information processing system looks like Figure 16.5.

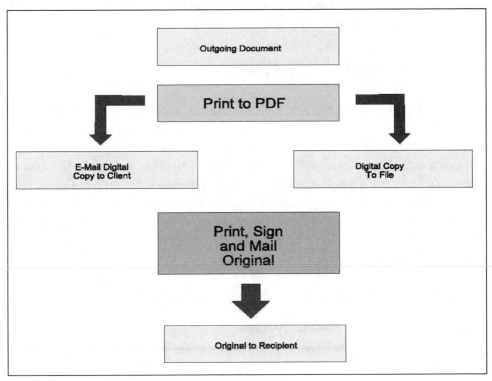

Figure 16.5

To move to a paperless office using Acrobat, you need follow only a few simple rules:

- ◆ **Rule Number One:** When a piece of paper comes into the office it goes through the scanner. This is a simple rule with few exceptions. Use Acrobat to convert paper to PDF (see Section 4.2).
- ◆ **Rule Number Two:** All items of outgoing work product are printed (converted) to PDF (see Section 4.1). Printing to PDF can be as simple as clicking a button on a toolbar that invokes the Adobe PDF print driver; you then select the folder where the PDF version of the document is stored. Printing to PDF differs from printing to a physical printer in that no toner or paper is used; otherwise, the final product (file copy) looks just like what would come out of a physical printer. In some cases, pleadings are filed electronically with the court, copies are served on the other parties by the filing service (either electronically or by mail), and a copy of the pleading is sent to the client as an attachment to an e-mail message. Looking at the process in this scenario, the work product never exists in paper form. Adherence to Rules Number One and Two generates a lot of PDF files and the need for the next rule.
- ◆ **Rule Number Three:** Store digital images of all incoming paper and outgoing work product in logical folders.

§ 16.4 The Digital Filing System

What system do you use right now, today, to find a given piece of paper? Perhaps it sounds something like this: Every client matter has a file, and somewhere you have an index of all those files (so if you want to find the Smith file and can't remember where in the filing system it resides, you go to the index, find the file identifier (such as a file number) and then locate the file. Now you know the document you want is in the Smith file—great—but what if the Smith file contains five thousand or ten thousand pages? At this point, the paper filing system starts to break down. How many subfolders are you willing to create, and how do you keep track of them? Unless you have an absolutely huge number of files, or a moderate number of really big files, then the paper filing system can be replicated, refined, and expanded in the digital world.

§ 16.4.1 The Logical Folder System

It may help to think of the digital filing system in terms of a physical filing system. The digital file room consists of electronic filing cabinets filled with folders that contain everything found in traditional paper files. Think of a shared hard disk drive as the file room. The cabinets within the room are large divisions on the disk; within those cabinet-size divisions are folders for each client matter. Most client matter folders are further divided into subfolders to aid in organization.

As high-tech as scanning and printing to PDF may sound, the storage and organizational system can adhere to an old-fashioned filing cabinet metaphor. The filing cabinet exists in virtual space (on a computer hard disk drive shared over a local area network). The filing cabinet has a name, Work (you may also want separate digital filing cabinets for Closed Files, Admin Files, and so on). Each computer on the network links to the filing cabinets by mapping one or more network drives, such as X:\Work. Now each desktop has access to the filing cabinet Work. Within the filing cabinet are folders, one for each client, such as X:\Work\Smith. If a client has several matters, then that client folder has a subfolder for each distinct matter, such as X:\Work\Smith\Corporation and X:\Work\Smith\Wills. Within each client matter folder are folders for various types of documents, such as correspondence, pleadings, expense receipts, research, privilege, and so on (see Figure 16.6, left pane).

A simple system for electronic filing can be implemented and standardized by creating a set of predefined subfolders for client matters. A standard set of folders can be created for litigation, transactional, or other types of matters.

In Figure 16.6, the main folder bears the name Litigation, meaning that this folder contains the file structure for new litigation matters. The subfolders in the Litigation folder are empty; when opening a new litigation file, simply highlight the Litigation folder, then select all (**Ctrl+A**), copy, and then paste this file structure onto the folder created for the new matter. Now, every litigation file has the same structure, at least to start with. As you can see, this file structure provides more detail than what you have been using in the paper world, and of course you can add all the subfolders you want and then simply drag and drop the contents from one folder to another. File reorganization can't be much easier.

§ 16.4.2 The Dual-Folder System

In order to maintain a digital file that looks like a paper file, consider using dual folders for correspondence and pleadings. One folder contains the native application files (Word, WordPerfect, Excel, and so on), and the other has the PDF versions. For example, correspondence files created with WordPerfect are stored in a subfolder named CorresWPD. All correspondence files in PDF format are stored in a subfolder called CorresPDF. A similar dual-folder system exists for pleadings.

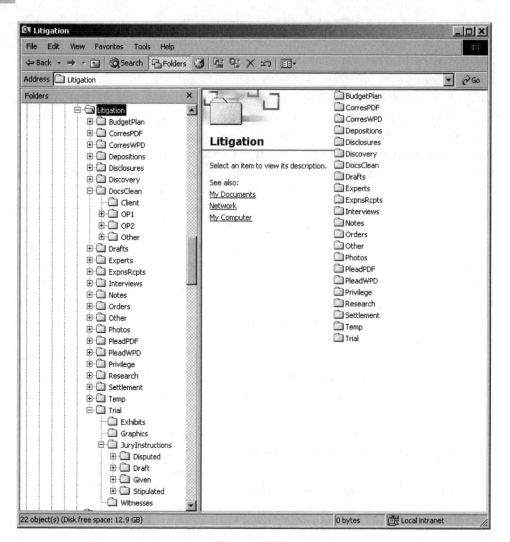

Figure 16.6

There are two reasons for maintaining dual folders. First, keeping the original work product in its native format allows for easy reuse. Second, the PDF folder acts like the old paper file; it contains all of the incoming and outgoing correspondence or pleadings, as the case may be. The files within the folders are named following a simple convention; see Section 16.4.3 below.

§ 16.4.3 File Naming Conventions

The logical folder system described above goes a long way toward organizing most document collections. But, to make sense of the documents within the folders, file naming conventions should be adopted and strictly adhered to. The files within the folders are named following simple conventions; the first part of the name always contains the date of the document in reverse year-month-day order, followed by a few descriptive terms, such as X:\Work\Smith\PleadPDF\020327 Complaint. By inserting the date at the beginning of the file name, all documents in a given folder are sorted in year-month-day order (see Figure 16.6, right pane). If the file being named (saved and filed) is an item of correspondence, consider using the date (in reverse order), followed by the initials of the author, followed by the initials of the recipient, followed by a short description (such as X:\Work\Smith\Corres\031-231 DLM MDH AmendedPrivLog). By using this convention for correspondence, you can quickly find letters by looking at the date, author, and recipient portion of the file name.

§ 16.4.4 The System in Action

Implementation of Rule Number One (when a piece of paper comes through the door it goes through the scanner) can be accomplished quite easily. The mail (correspondence, pleadings, bills, and so on) goes to an assistant who scans each piece, stores the image to the appropriate client or administrative folder, and then distributes the paper to the proper recipient within the office (lawyer, paralegal, bookkeeper) for action. For example, when a letter arrives from opposing counsel, it goes through the scanner, and then goes to the proper recipient within the office. A letter is written to the client that discusses the enclosure that typically begins, "Enclosed for your review and records please find an item of correspondence that we received from opposing counsel. We have retained a copy in our records." Following this procedure, paper comes in, goes through the scanner, then goes out to the client. In some cases, with the right client, you simply send an e-mail message and attach a digital copy; the original letter then goes to the recycle bin or shredder.

Following a few simple rules, any office can switch from paper to digital filing: (1) scan all incoming documents to PDF, (2) print all outgoing work product to PDF, (3) create a virtual filing cabinet with folders for each client matter, (4) segregate document types within the client matter folders into appropriate subfolders, and (5) use dates or a numbering system when naming files so that they display in chronological order.

§ 16.4.5 Document Management Alternatives

If the document management system described above does not sound robust enough for your office, consider an industrial-strength solution. However, if all you want is a system that indexes all of your files so that you can run a computer search to find the Smith lease, or locate that motion to compel a psychiatric examination, you already have it—it's called Windows Explorer. You can use Windows Explorer to find files containing specific words (Acrobat document summaries and notes are included in the information searched by Explorer). If you need more than Windows Explorer can deliver, then consider Worldox or iManage. They provide industrial-strength file management (at a price, of course—not just in dollars, but in training and in following a regimented system of coding files). In the middle, between Windows Explorer and industrial-strength, are case management programs (or groupware) like Amicus Attorney, Time Matters, and GroupWise. These programs have document management capabilities, some more than others. Try implementing a good logical in-house electronic file system like that illustrated above; if you can't find your documents with that system (aided by Windows Explorer when the going gets rough), then look at document management system applications like Worldox and iManage. Remember, when you create a large collection of PDF image-on-text files, you can index the collection, which then allows you to search the entire collection.

§ 16.5 Digital Document Storage Requirements

As a general rule, when scanned at 300 dpi, a single scanned page (letter size) requires storage space of approximately 50 KB. This is an average and assumes the image was acquired and stored as black and white or line drawing, not color or gray scale. A single drawer in a filing cabinet holds approximately ten thousand pages. To store the same ten thousand pages electronically requires 500 megabytes (MB) of storage space. A single compact disc (CD-ROM, CD-R, or CD-RW) holds 700 MB, or the equivalent of 1.4 file cabinet drawers. An entire four-drawer filing cabinet (forty thousand pages) then requires only 2 gigabytes (GB). Although there are standards issues yet to be resolved, prices for DVD writers have approached the reasonable range, with many under $300. A single DVD holds 4.3 GB, or the equivalent of two four-drawer filing cabinets. 80-GB hard disk drives currently sell for less than $100; that's the capacity of forty four-drawer filing cabinets. If you think in terms of boxes, instead of filing cabinets, one box holds approximately 2,500 pages. Those same 2,500 pages require only 125 MB of digital storage space. Five boxes of documents fit on a single CD-ROM with room to spare. Even if the space required for a single page, scanned at 300 dpi, was doubled to 100 KB, ten thousand pages (one full file cabinet drawer or four boxes) require only 1 GB of electronic storage capacity.

The available space for digital document storage continues to grow while prices continue to drop. Contrast that with the fixed physical space for storing paper files and the continual increasing costs of such storage. Document collections should be stored on a network drive, either an internal hard disk drive or a storage appliance such as a Snap Drive. When planning or acquiring storage devices, consider the speed at which documents can be retrieved. Fast hard disk drives (7,200 RPM or 10,000 RPM) are much preferred. If stored documents are available across a network, fast Ethernet (100 MB/second) provides good performance. Standard Ethernet (10 MB/second) and 801.11(b) wireless (11 MB/second) do not provide sufficient bandwidth if you create large scanned documents (documents in excess of a thousand pages).

The discussion of storage space requirements to this point has addressed only scanned documents. Documents printed to PDF require much less storage space. For example, a six-page word processing document 30 KB in size grew to 70 KB when printed to PDF, but would have been 300 KB if scanned.

Resources and Glossary 17

Resources

Web Sites

www.adobe.com
www.planetpdf.com
www.pdfzone.com
www.appeligent.com
www.intellipdf.com

Books

How to Do Everything with Adobe Acrobat 6.0 (Windows) by Doug Sahlin (June 2003)

Adobe Acrobat 6.0 Pro Classroom in a Book by Adobe Creative Team (March 2004)

Adobe Acrobat 6 PDF Bible by Ted Padova and Sarah Rosenbaum (October 2003)

Adobe Acrobat 6 PDF for Dummies by Greg Harvey (July 2003)

The 100 Best Adobe Acrobat 6 Tips and Tricks by Donna Baker (September 2003)

Adobe Acrobat 6.0 Standard Classroom in a Book by Adobe Creative Team (August 2003)

Real World Adobe Acrobat Pro 6 by Christopher Smith, et al (September 2003)

Adobe Acrobat 6: The Professional User's Guide by Tom Carson and Donna L. Baker (December 2003)

Adobe Acrobat 6 Complete Course by Ted Padova (January 2003)

Glossary

Acrobat—Adobe Acrobat is the cornerstone of the Acrobat family of products; it enables you to create and work with PDF files.

Acrobat Capture—(not the same as Capture Pages) A Microsoft Windows OLE server application that is designed for the batch conversion of image files to PDF and the recognition of the text to create searchable-text PDF files.

Acrobat Distiller—Acts as a PostScript interpreter that can be used to convert PostScript to PDF. Distiller is intended for the use and for the creation of PDF files containing high-end print publishing features.

Adobe Reader—Reader is a free application, readily available on the Internet, with which anyone can open, display, search, and print PDF documents. Reader does not allow you to add bookmarks, notes, links, or most of the other features that make Acrobat a valuable tool in the law office.

Batch Processing—A defined series of commands with specific settings and in a specific order, applied in a single step. You can apply a sequence to a single document, to several documents, or to an entire collection of documents.

Bates Number—Bates numbering, or Bates stamping, refers to numbering each page of a document with a unique number. Bates numbers allow lawyers to keep track of all documents produced or received during the course of litigation. The numbers increase by one digit on each page and used to be applied to paper documents using a hand stamp machine originally manufactured by the Bates Manufacturing Company.

BMP—A standard format for graphic files in Windows. BMP stands for bit-mapped graphic.

Bookmark—A type of link created within a document to aid navigation.

Capture Pages or **Paper Capture**—An optical character recognition (OCR) feature within Acrobat that converts image-only PDF files to image-on-text PDF files.

Catalog—A feature of Acrobat that creates an index of image-on-text PDF files that allows for faster and more advanced searches.

Comments—A comment refers to a note, highlighting, and any other markup added to a PDF document using the Commenting tools. Notes are the most commonly used comment.

Crop—A function of Acrobat that allows users to trim away portions of a page (think scissors).

Digital Signature—A secure mechanism for signing electronic documents.

Find (Ctrl+F)—The Acrobat function that allows searching within the current PDF file.

Headers and Footers—Much like headers and footers in word processing, an area at the top and bottom of a document where text can be added that appears on all or some pages.

Image-only PDF file—Image-only PDFs are just that—images only—digital photocopies of paper documents.

Image-on-text PDF file—Image-on-text files have an exact image of the hard copy with text behind the image. Image-on-text files are created by printing an existing computer file to PDF (word processing and spreadsheet files are good examples), or by running a PDF image-only file through an optical character recognition (OCR) application.

JPEG—An image file format commonly used on the Web. JPEG stands for Joint Pictures Expert Group, the committee that developed the format. JPEG images are compressed, with some loss of image quality.

Links—You can use links to jump to another location in a document, to another document, or to a Web site (think links on Web pages).

Menu Bar or **Menus**—The topmost row of items in the Acrobat window. There are six menus: File, Edit, View, Document, Tools, Advanced, Window, and Help.

PDF—Portable Document Format—thus we speak of PDF files or PDF documents, but not PDF *format* files.

PDF Writer—Emulates a printer driver and converts the GDI or Quickdraw commands from Windows and Macintosh applications to PDF documents. PDF Writer is intended for desktop applications.

Plug-ins—Dynamically linked extensions to Adobe Acrobat or Adobe Acrobat Reader. These programs add greater functionality to the products that they plug into.

OCR—(Optical Character Recognition) OCR applications look at image-only files and convert the numbers, letters, and symbols within the image to a text file format. The Capture Pages feature within Acrobat is an OCR application that converts image-only PDF files to image-on-text PDF files.

Search (Ctrl+F)—Same as Find.

Stamp—A tool for quickly adding content to PDF documents. Think rubber stamps.

Task Buttons—The buttons on the toolbars for performing tasks.

TIFF—Tagged Image File Format, a bit-mapped image file format commonly used for high-resolution images, especially in desktop publishing and graphics programs.

Toolbars—The row or rows of buttons directly below the menus. You can display some or all toolbars. To quickly display all toolbars, right-click in the toolbar area and select Dock All Toolbars.

Web Capture—An Acrobat tool that opens Web pages and converts them to PDF files.

Index

**The Lawyer's Guide to Fact Finding
on the Internet, Second Edition**
By Carole A. Levitt and Mark E. Rosch
Written especially for legal professionals, this revised and expanded edition is a complete hands-on guide to the best sites, secrets, and shortcuts for conducting efficient research on the Web. Containing over 600 pages of information, with over 100 screen shots of specific Web sites, this resource is filled with practical tips and advice on using specific sites, alerting readers to quirks or hard-to-find information. What's more, user-friendly icons immediately identify free sites, free-with-registration sites, and pay sites. An accompanying CD-ROM includes the links contained in the book, indexed, so you can easily navigate to these cream-of-the-crop Web sites without typing URLs into your browser.

**Subscribe to *The Lawyer's Guide to
Fact Finding on the Internet* E-Newsletter to
stay current on the most valuable Web sites!**
Each issue contains ten sites specifically chosen for their usefulness to legal professionals. Simply the best way to stay on top of Web sites that are important to you.

The Lawyer's Guide to Palm Powered™ Handhelds
By Margaret Spencer Dixon
The Palm-powered handheld is now an essential part of everyday life for an increasing number of lawyers. Whether you are a beginner, an advanced user, or simply deciding whether a Palm® PDA is right for you, this book will show you how a Palm-powered handheld can make you more efficient and effective at what you do. Written by a lawyer for lawyers, this guidebook provides helpful tips and tricks for getting the most out of Palm applications. Learn to take full advantage of your Palm Powered™ handheld to manage addresses, appointments, expenses, and time; write memos; take notes; check e-mail; read books and documents; and much more. In addition, you'll find a wealth of suggested Web sites and handy tips from top legal power users. If you're a lawyer searching for a book to get you up and running on the Palm platform and become a Palm power-user, look no further!

**The Lawyer's Guide to Extranets:
Breaking Down Walls, Building Client Connections**
by Douglas Simpson and Mark Tamminga
An extranet can be a powerful tool that allows law firms to exchange information and build relationships with clients. This new book shows you why extranets are the next step in client interaction and communications, and how you can effectively implement an extranet in any type of firm. This book will take you step-by-step through the issues of implementing an extranet, and how to plan and build one.

**The Lawyer's Guide to Marketing on the Internet,
Second Edition**
*By Gregory H. Siskind, Deborah McMurray, and
Richard P. Klau*
The Internet is a critical component of every law firm marketing strategy—no matter where you are, how large your firm is, or the areas in which you practice. Used effectively, a younger, smaller firm can present an image just as sophisticated and impressive as a larger and more established firm. You can reach potential new clients, in remote areas, at any time, for minimal cost. Learn the latest and most effective ways to create and implement a successful Internet marketing strategy for your firm, including what elements you need to consider and the options that are available to you now.

**The Lawyer's Guide to Strategic Planning:
Defining, Setting, and Achieving Your Firm's Goals**
By Thomas C. Grella and Michael L. Hudkins
This practice-building resource is your guide to planning dynamic strategic plans and implementing them at your firm. You'll learn about the actual planning process and how to establish goals in key planning areas such as law firm governance, competition, opening a new office, financial management, technology, marketing and competitive intelligence, client development and retention, and more. The accompanying CD-ROM contains a wealth of policies, statements, and questionnaires. If you're serious about improving the way your firm works, increasing productivity, making better decisions, and setting your firm on the right course—this book is the resource you need.

The Lawyer's Guide to Summation®
by Tom O'Connor
Summation gives you complete control over litigation evidence by bringing all you need—transcripts, documents, issues and events—to your fingertips in one easy-to-use software program. Working in close collaboration with Summation® Legal Technologies, Inc., author and noted legal technologist Tom O'Connor has developed this easy-to-understand guide designed to quickly get you up and running on Summation software. Fully up to date, covering the latest version of Summation, the book features step-by-step instructions on the functions of Summation, and shows you how to get the most from this powerful program. Helpful screenshots throughout illustrate all the procedures being discussed, and "Practice Pointer" sidebars illustrate the processes where Summation can make the task of managing litigation more efficient for you.

**How to Start and Build a Law Practice,
Platinum Fifth Edition**
By Jay G Foonberg
This classic ABA bestseller—now completely updated—is the primary resource for starting your own firm. This acclaimed book covers all aspects of getting started, including finding clients, determining the right location, setting fees, buying office equipment, maintaining an ethical and responsible practice, maximizing available resources, upholding your standards, and marketing your practice, just to name a few. In addition, you'll find a business plan template, forms, checklists, sample letters, and much more. A must for any lawyer just starting out—or growing—a solo practice.

Marketing Success Stories:
Conversations with Leading Lawyers
Hollis Hatfield Weishar and Joyce K. Smiley
This practice-building resource is an insightful collection of anecdotes on successful and creative marketing techniques used by lawyers and marketing professionals in a variety of practice settings. Whether you work in a solo, mid-sized, or mega-firm, these stories of marketing strategies that paid off will inspire you to greater heights. In addition to dozens of first-hand accounts of success stories from practitioners, you won't want to miss the advice from in-house counsel who give candid feedback on how strategic marketing influences their decision to hire a specific firm. Readers will also learn how to make new contacts, gain more repeat business, increase their visibility within the community, and many other action steps to take.

Compensation Plans for Law Firms, Fourth Edition
Edited by James D. Cotterman, Altman Weil, Inc.
In this newly revised and updated fourth edition, you'll find complete and systematic guidance on how to establish workable plans for compensating partners and associates, as well as other contributors to the firm. Discover how to align your firm's compensation plans with your culture, business objectives, and market realities. The book features valuable data from leading legal consulting firm Altman Weil's annual and triennial surveys on law firm performance and compensation, retirement, and withdrawal and compensation systems. You'll see where your firm stands on salaries and bonuses, as well as benefit from detailed analyses of compensation plans for everyone in your firm.

Results-Oriented Financial Management:
A Step-By-Step Guide to Law Firm Profitability, Second Edition
By John G. Iezzi, CPA
This hands-on, how-to book will assist managing partners, law firm managers, and law firm accountants by providing them with the budgeting and financial knowledge they need to need to make the critical decisions. Whether you're a financial novice or veteran manager, this book will help you examine every facet of your financial affairs from cash flow and budget creation to billing and compensation. Also included with the book are valuable financial models on CD-ROM allowing you to compute profitability and determine budgets by inputting your own data. The appendix contains useful forms and examples from lawyers who have actually implemented alternative billing methods at their firms.

Paralegals, Profitability, and the Future of Your Law Practice
By Arthur G. Greene and Therese A. Cannon
This is your essential guide to effectively integrating paralegals into your practice and expanding their roles to ensure your firm is successful in the next decade. If you're not currently using paralegals in your firm, authors Arthur G. Greene and Therese A. Cannon explain why you need paralegals and how to create a paralegal model for use in your firm—no matter what the size or structure. You'll learn how to recruit and hire top-notch paralegals the first time. If you are currently using paralegals, you'll learn how to make sure your paralegal program is structured properly, runs effectively, and continually contributes to your bottom line. In addition, all the forms and guidelines contained in the appendix are included on a CD-ROM for ease in implementation!

The Lawyer's Guide to Marketing Your Practice, Second Edition
Edited by James A. Durham and Deborah McMurray
This book is packed with practical ideas, innovative strategies, useful checklists, and sample marketing and action plans to help you implement a successful, multifaceted, and profit-enhancing marketing plan for your firm. Organized into four sections, this illuminating resource covers: Developing Your Approach; Enhancing Your Image; Implementing Marketing Strategies, and Maintaining Your Program. Appendix materials include an instructive primer on market research to inform you on research methodologies that support the marketing of legal services. The accompanying CD-ROM contains a wealth of checklists, plans, and other sample reports, questionnaires, and templates—all designed to make implementing your marketing strategy as easy as possible!

LawPracticeManagementSection
MARKETING • MANAGEMENT • TECHNOLOGY • FINANCE

TO ORDER CALL TOLL-FREE:
1-800-285-2221

VISIT OUR WEB SITE:
www.lawpractice.org/catalog

30-Day Risk-Free Order Form
Call Today! 1-800-285-2221
Monday–Friday, 7:30 AM – 5:30 PM, Central Time

Qty	Title	LPM Price	Regular Price	Total
_____	The Lawyer's Guide to Fact Finding on the Internet, Second Edition (5110497)	$69.95	$79.95	$_____
_____	The Lawyer's Guide to Fact Finding on the Internet E-mail Newsletter (5110498)	37.95	44.95	$_____
_____	The Lawyer's Guide to Palm Powered™ Handhelds (5110505)	54.95	64.95	$_____
_____	The Lawyer's Guide to Extranets (5110494)	59.95	69.95	$_____
_____	The Lawyer's Guide to Marketing on the Internet, Second Edition (5110484)	69.95	79.95	$_____
_____	The Lawyer's Guide to Strategic Planning (5110520)	59.95	79.95	$_____
_____	The Lawyer's Guide to Summation (5110510)	29.95	34.95	$_____
_____	How to Start and Build a Law Practice, Platinum Fifth Edition (5110508)	57.95	69.95	$_____
_____	Marketing Success Stories: Conversations with Leading Lawyers, Second Edition (5110511)	64.95	74.95	$_____
_____	Compensation Plans for Law Firms, Fourth Edition (5110507)	79.95	94.95	$_____
_____	Results-Oriented Financial Management, Second Edition (5110493)	89.95	99.95	$_____
_____	Paralegals, Profitability, and the Future of Your Law Practice (5110491)	59.95	69.95	$_____
_____	The Lawyer's Guide to Marketing Your Practice, Second Edition (5110500)	79.95	89.95	$_____

*Postage and Handling	
$10.00 to $24.99	$5.95
$25.00 to $49.99	$9.95
$50.00 to $99.99	$12.95
$100.00 to $349.99	$17.95
$350 to $499.99	$24.95

**Tax
DC residents add 5.75%
IL residents add 8.75%
MD residents add 5%

*Postage and Handling	$_____
**Tax	$_____
TOTAL	$_____

PAYMENT

❑ Check enclosed (to the ABA)

❑ Visa   ❑ MasterCard   ❑ American Express

_____
Account Number   Exp. Date   Signature

Name _____ Firm _____
Address _____
City _____ State _____ Zip _____
Phone Number _____ E-Mail Address _____

Note: E-Mail address is required if ordering the
The Lawyer's Guide to Fact Finding on the Internet
E-mail Newsletter (5110498)

Guarantee
If—for any reason—you are not satisfied with your purchase, you may
return it within 30 days of receipt for a complete refund of the price of the
book(s). No questions asked!

Mail: ABA Publication Orders, P.O. Box 10892, Chicago, Illinois 60610-0892
◆ **Phone: 1-800-285-2221** ◆ **FAX: 312-988-5568**

E-Mail: abasvcctr@abanet.org ◆ **Internet: http://www.lawpractice.org/catalog**

LawPracticeManagementSection

MARKETING • MANAGEMENT • TECHNOLOGY • FINANCE

JOIN the ABA Law Practice Management Section (LPM) and receive significant discounts on future LPM book purchases! You'll also get direct access to marketing, management, technology, and finance tools that help lawyers and other professionals meet the demands of today's challenging legal environment.

Exclusive Membership Benefits Include:

- **Law Practice Magazine**
  Eight annual issues of our award-winning *Law Practice* magazine, full of insightful articles and practical tips on Marketing/Client Development, Practice Management, Legal Technology, and Finance.
- **ABA TECHSHOW®**
  Receive a $100 discount on ABA TECHSHOW, the world's largest legal technology conference!
- **LPM Book Discount**
  LPM has over eighty titles in print! Books topics cover the four core areas of law practice management – marketing, management, technology, and finance – as well as legal career issues.
- **Law Practice Today**
  LPM's unique web-based magazine in which the features change weekly! Law Practice Today covers all the hot topics in law practice management *today* – current issues, current challenges, current solutions.
- **Discounted CLE & Other Educational Opportunities**
  The Law Practice Management Section sponsors more than 100 educational sessions annually. LPM also offers other live programs, teleconferences and web cast seminars.
- **LawPractice.news**
  This monthly eUpdate brings information on Section news and activities, educational opportunities, and details on book releases and special offers.

Complete the membership application below.

Applicable Dues:
o$40 for ABA members   o$5 for ABA Law Student Division members

(ABA Membership is a prerequisite to membership in the Section. To join the ABA, call the Service Center at 1-800-285-2221.)

Method of Payment:
oBill me   Charge to my: oVisa   oMasterCard   oAmerican Express
Card number _____   Exp. Date _____
Signature _____   Date _____

Applicant's Information (please print):
Name _____ ABA I.D. number _____
Firm/Organization _____
Address _____ City/State/Zip _____
Telephone _____ FAX _____ Email _____

Fax your application to 312-988-5528 or join by phone: 1-800-285-2221, TDD 312-988-5168
Join online at www.lawpractice.org.

I understand that my membership dues include $16 for a basic subscription to *Law Practice Management* magazine. This subscription charge is not deductible from the dues and additional subscriptions are not available at this rate. Membership dues in the American Bar Association and its Sections are not deductible as charitable contributions for income tax purposes but may be deductible as a business expense.